MATH SERIES

PRE-CALCULUS

by Stan VerNooy

Dedicated to George Hawley,
and in memory of Chester Bodkin and William Hempstead.

Published by
Garlic Press
605 Powers St.
Eugene, OR 97402

ISBN 0-931993-53-9
Order Number GP-053

www.garlicpress.com

Pre-Calculus
Introduction

This book covers the material which is traditionally contained in a high school or college pre-calculus class. It covers advanced topics in algebra and trigonometry. An understanding of this material is necessary before beginning either the standard college calculus or high school AP calculus courses. The reader is assumed to be familiar with the contents of **Straight Forward Algebra** (Books 1 and 2) and **Straight Forward Trigonometry**.

Table of Contents

Preliminary Ideas

This chapter covers some mathematical ideas which the reader will need to know before proceeding on to the rest of the book and which were not covered in the **Straight Forward Math Series** before.

Part 1	Interval Notation

Interval notation is a convenient way to describe a continuous range of numbers. To describe the set of all real numbers between 2 and 7 (not including 2 and 7), we use the notation (2,7). If we want to include either the number 2 or the number 7 in the set, we use a square bracket on the side of the number we want to include.

•Example:

> Express the set of all numbers greater than or equal to -3 and smaller than 10 in interval notation.
>
> SOLUTION: [-3,10)
>
> A square bracket is on the left because -3 is included in our interval. A round bracket on the right to indicates that 10 is <u>not</u> included in the interval.

NOTE: the notation for the interval from 3 to 8 is the same as the notation for the point on a graph where the x-coordinate is 3 and the y-coordinate is 8. We use (3, 8) in both cases. Usually this should not cause confusion, because the context will make it obvious whether we are talking about an interval or a point.

When we want to describe the set of all numbers greater than or less than some particular number, we use the symbols for infinity (∞) or minus infinity (-∞) as the upper or lower endpoint of the interval.

•Examples:

Describe the following sets of numbers in interval notation:
     a. All numbers less than 6.21.
     b. All numbers greater than or equal to 4.
     c. All numbers less than or equal to $-\frac{93}{16}$.
     d. All positive numbers.

SOLUTION: a. $(-\infty, 6.21)$ c. $(-\infty, -\frac{93}{16}]$

            b. $[4, \infty)$ d. $(0, \infty)$

Note that we never use a square bracket at an interval end which has a plus or minus infinity.

Terminology: An interval with rounded brackets is called *open*.
                    An interval with square brackets is called *closed*.
                    An interval with one round bracket and one square bracket is called *half-open*.

Intervals and Number Lines

A round bracket in interval notation corresponds to an open dot on a number line; a square bracket in interval notation corresponds to a solid dot on a number line.

•Examples:

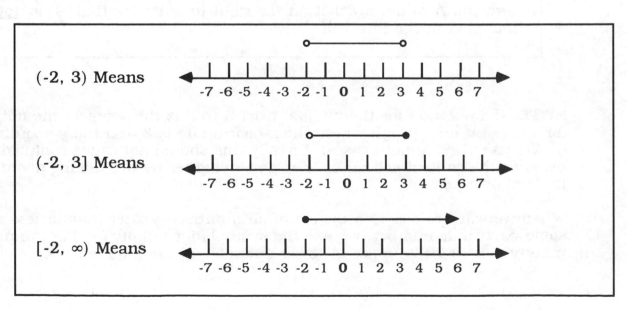

Unions of Intervals

If we want to describe a set of numbers which includes two intervals, we write the two intervals with the notation ∪ in between them.

•Example:

> Write the interval notations for:
>   a. The set of numbers which includes the intervals
>   (-6, 0) and [2, ∞).
>   b. The set of numbers which includes all real numbers except 7.
>
> Solution: a. (-6, 0) ∪ [2, ∞)
>   b. (-∞ , 7) ∪ (7, ∞)
>
> Part (b) illustrates a common method for describing the set of all real numbers except one specified number.

Preliminary Ideas, Exercise 1, Interval Notations.

1. Write interval notation for the sets designated on each number line:

a

b.

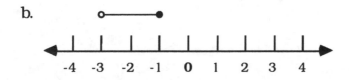

c.

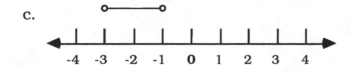

d.

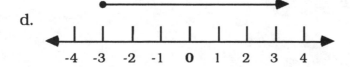

e.

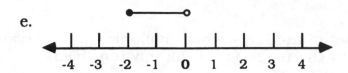

f.

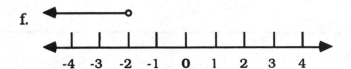

2. Write interval notation for the sets of x's described by the inequalities below:

    a. x < 4
    b. x ≥ 0
    c. 0 < x ≤ 5
    d. -2 ≤ x < 1
    e. 0 < x < 1
    f. -2 ≤ x ≤ 5

3. Draw each interval on a number line:

    a. (-2, -1)
    b. (-1, 0]
    c. [0, 1)
    d. [1, 2]
    e. (-∞, 2)
    f. [2, ∞)

4. For each interval, write an inequality which is equivalent to saying that x is in the interval:

    a. (-5, -3)
    b. [-2, 6]
    c. (0, 3)
    d. [-5, 0)
    e. (-∞, 0]
    f. (5, ∞)

Part 2

Absolute Value

The absolute value of a number is just the number itself, with the minus sign removed if the number is negative. Therefore, *the absolute value of a number can never be negative.*

We denote the absolute value of any number by placing straight vertical lines on either side of the number:

$$|-5| = \text{absolute value of -5} = 5$$

•Examples:

$$|-23| = 23$$

$$|23| = 23$$

$$|0| = 0$$

Another way to think of the absolute value of a number is that the absolute value measures the distance between a number and zero on a number line:

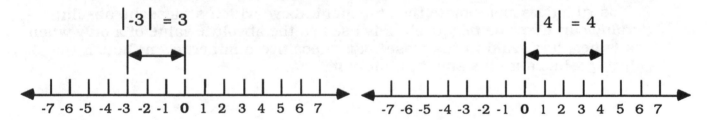

More facts worth remembering about absolute values:

1. Any number and the negative of that number have the same absolute value:

$$|x| = |-x|$$

2. The absolute value of a negative number is the negative (or opposite) of the original negative number:

$$|-6| = -(-6) = 6$$

3. Another way of defining absolute value is:

$$|x| = \sqrt{x^2}$$

5

This works because the square of any number is positive and the $\sqrt{}$ sign always gives the <u>positive</u> square root.

4. For any numbers a and b, the absolute value $|a - b|$ gives the distance between a and b in either direction on a number line:

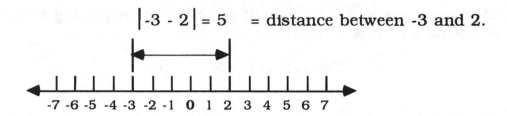

$$|-3 - 2| = 5 \quad = \text{distance between -3 and 2.}$$

Absolute Value of an Algebraic Expression

When we use the letter x to designate an undetermined number, we don't know whether x stands for a positive or a negative number. So sometimes we define the absolute value of a variable x by saying:

$$|x| = x \quad \text{if } x \geq 0$$

$$|x| = -x \quad \text{if } x < 0$$

This rule does not violate the statement above which states: the absolute value can never be negative! -x is used as the absolute value of x only when x is negative. And in that case, -x is a positive number, even though the <u>letter</u> x has a minus sign in front of it.

•Examples:

If x = 6, then $\quad |x| = x = 6$

If x = - 6, then $\quad |x| = -x = -(-6) = 6$

The same idea can be applied to the absolute value of a more complicated expression.

6

•Example:

Express $|2x - 14|$ without the absolute value notation.

SOLUTION:

$|2x - 14| = 2x - 14$ when $2x - 14$ is positive or zero, and
$|2x - 14| = -(2x - 14) = -2x + 14$ when $2x - 14$ is negative. So we need to find out what values of x make the expression $2x - 14$ negative.

First, we remember that "negative" means the same thing as "less than zero". So what we really want to do is solve the inequality:
$$2x - 14 < 0$$

By applying the usual rules for solving inequalities, we get:

$$2x - 14 < 0$$
$$2x < 14$$
$$x < 7$$

So, $2x - 14 < 0$ whenever $x < 7$, and $2x - 14 \geq 0$ if $x \geq 7$.

Therefore:

$$|2x - 14| = 2x - 14 \text{ when } x \geq 7, \text{ and}$$
$$-2x + 14 \text{ when } x < 7.$$

Equations Involving Absolute Values

If the absolute value of some algebraic expression is equal to 4, for example, the value of the expression itself might be equal to plus 4 <u>or</u> minus 4. This gives us a method for solving simple equations with absolute values in them.

•Example:

Solve: $|2x - 6| = 4$.

SOLUTION:

This equation will be true if $2x - 6 = 4$, and it will also be true if

7

2x - 6 = -4. So we have two solutions, one from each equation:

$$2x - 6 = 4 \qquad\qquad 2x - 6 = -4$$
$$2x = 10 \qquad\qquad 2x = 2$$
$$x = 5 \qquad\qquad x = 1$$

So, x = 5 and x = 1 are both solutions of the original equation.

Preliminary Ideas, Exercise 2. Absolute Value.

1. Express without absolute value sign:

   a. $|x|$ c. $|10 - x|$ e. $|-6 - 2x|$
   b. $|-x|$ d. $|3x + 10|$

2. Find the value of the following expressions when x = -2. Use two different methods: first, write the given expression without the absolute value signs and then substitute x = -2; and second, substitute x = -2 into the expression first and then find the absolute value:

   a. $|x|$ c. $|x + 1|$ e. $|5x - 10|$
   b. $|-x|$ d. $|x + 2|$ f. $|2x + 3|$

3. Solve the following equations:

   a. $|2x| = 8$ c. $|2x - 5| = 5$ e. $|2x - 5| = x + 1$ g. $|3x - 5| = x - 7$
   b. $|x - 5| = 5$ d. $|2x - 5| = -5$ f. $|3x - 5| = 3x + 11$ h. $|3 - 2x| = x + 3$

Part 3   nth Roots and Fractional Exponents

As we know, the square root of a number x is a number which, when squared, gives us x. Instead of using the word "squared", we can say:

> The <u>2nd</u> root of a number x is a number which, when raised to the <u>2nd</u> power, gives us x.

Once we have defined a 2nd root as in the statement above, we can define the 3rd, 4th, or 28th roots of a number in the same way:

> If n is a positive integer, an nth root of a number x is a number which, when raised to the nth power, gives us x.

8

•Examples:

> 4 is a 3rd root (sometimes called a *cube* root) of 64.
>
> Both 2 and -2 are 8th roots of 256.
>
> -1 is a 5th root of -1.
>
> -1 is a 9997th root of -1 (Yeah, really!)
>
> There are no real 12th roots of -1.

We already know that $\sqrt{x}$ refers to the square root (or 2nd root) of x. By placing a number n in the little notch at the front of the $\sqrt{}$ sign (the $\sqrt{}$ sign is called a <u>radical</u>), the meaning of $\sqrt[n]{}$ becomes:

> $\sqrt[n]{x}$ = the (principal) nth root of x.

The *principal* nth root means that we use the positive root whenever there are both positive and negative numbers which would work. This definition means that the original radical without a number ($\sqrt{}$) is the same as $\sqrt[2]{}$.

Important facts:

    a. If n is even, then $\sqrt[n]{x}$ exists only if x is positive or zero (because you can't multiply something by itself an even number of times and end up with a negative).

    b. If n is even (and x is positive), then $\sqrt[n]{x}$ is <u>always</u> positive, even though there will be both a positive and a negative nth root.

    c. If n is odd, then $\sqrt[n]{x}$ exists whether x is positive or negative.

    d. If n is odd and x is negative, then $\sqrt[n]{x}$ is negative.

    e. If n is odd and x is positive, then $\sqrt[n]{x}$ is positive.

•Examples:

$\sqrt[4]{-16}$ does not exist in the real number system.

$\sqrt[8]{256}$ = 2 (Not - 2).

$\sqrt[3]{-125}$ = -5.

$\sqrt[3]{125}$ = 5.

Of course, for most numbers, the nth root is not a nice clean integer. But $\sqrt[n]{x}$ still exists, unless x is negative and n is even. For example, $\sqrt{2}$ is *approximately* equal to 1.4142135623773, but the actual value would go out to an infinite number of decimal places. In fact, it is impossible to write the exact value of $\sqrt{2}$ as a fraction with an integer on top and an integer on the bottom. A number which cannot be expressed as such a fraction is called *irrational*.

Fractional Exponents

In addition to using a radical sign with a number in the notch, we can express nth roots with exponents. Here is the rule:

$$x^{\frac{1}{n}} = \text{the principal nth root of x.}$$

The reason this rule works is easily seen. We already know that

$$(x^a)^b = x^{ab}$$

Therefore, $(x^{\frac{1}{n}})^n = x^1 = x$

In other words, $x^{\frac{1}{n}}$ is the number which, when raised to the nth power, gives us x. That is to say, $x^{\frac{1}{n}}$ is the nth root of x.

Finally, we can interpret any fractional exponent in the following way:

$$x^{\frac{a}{b}} = \sqrt[b]{x^a}$$
$$= (\sqrt[b]{x})^a$$

10

This works because of the power rule:

$$(x^a)^{\frac{1}{b}} = (x^{\frac{1}{b}})^a = x^{\frac{a}{b}}$$

Therefore:

$$x^{\frac{a}{b}} = (x^{\frac{1}{b}})^a = (\sqrt[b]{x})^a$$
$$= (x^a)^{\frac{1}{b}} = \sqrt[b]{x^a}$$

•Example:

Find: a. $9^{\frac{3}{2}}$

b. $(-8)^{\frac{2}{3}}$

c. $1000^{-\frac{2}{3}}$

SOLUTION:

a. $9^{\frac{3}{2}} = \left(\sqrt{9}\right)^3 = 3^3 = 27$

b. $(-8)^{\frac{2}{3}} = \left(\sqrt[3]{-8}\right)^2 = (-2)^2 = 4$

c. $1000^{-\frac{2}{3}} = \left(\sqrt[3]{1000}\right)^{-2} = 10^{-2} = \frac{1}{10^2} = \frac{1}{100}$

Preliminary Ideas, Exercise 3. nth Roots and Fractional Exponents.

Calculate the values of the following:

1. $9^{\frac{1}{2}}$

2. $(-9)^{\frac{1}{2}}$

3. $-9^{\frac{1}{2}}$

4. $8^{\frac{1}{3}}$

5. $(-8)^{\frac{1}{3}}$

6. $-8^{\frac{1}{3}}$

7. $9^{\frac{1}{2}} - (-8)^{\frac{1}{3}}$

8. $\sqrt{64}$

9. $\sqrt{-64}$

10. $\sqrt[3]{64}$

11. $\sqrt[3]{-64}$

12. $\sqrt[3]{x-2}$ when x = 29

13. $\sqrt[3]{2-x}$ when x = 29

14. $(x+4)^{\frac{1}{4}}$ when x = -4

15. $8^{\frac{5}{3}}$

16. $16^{\frac{3}{2}}$

17. $27^{-\frac{2}{3}}$

18. $(-8)^{\frac{5}{3}}$

19. $(-16)^{\frac{3}{2}}$

20. $(x-4)^{\frac{3}{4}}$ when x = 20

11

Complex Numbers

In addition to traditional real numbers, a new number has been invented and designated by an italicized i. It is defined to be the principal square root of -1. By adding the number i to our number system, we are able to include square roots of all negative numbers.

•Examples:

$$\sqrt{-9} = \sqrt{9}\ \sqrt{-1} = 3i$$
$$\sqrt{-13} = \sqrt{13}\ \sqrt{-1} = \sqrt{13}i$$

There are several important sets of numbers with which the reader should already be familar:

1. **Integers**. These are the "whole numbers", positive and negative. 1, 98, -5, and 0 are all integers.

2. **Rational numbers**. These are fractions formed from the integers. The integers themselves are rational numbers, because, for example, 7 is equal to $\frac{7}{1}$. Some rational numbers are: $\frac{3}{4}$, $\frac{-4}{3}$, 0, and $\frac{16}{11}$.

3. **Real numbers**. This set includes all of the "standard" numbers with which we are familar, including the rational numbers, along with numbers which cannot be expressed as one integer divided by another, such as $\sqrt{2}$ and π.

We now add the following two sets of numbers:

4. **Imaginary numbers.** An **imaginary number** is the number i multiplied by any real number. For example, i, $-17i$, $2.76i$, and $\sqrt{5}\ i$ are imaginary numbers.

5. **Complex numbers.** A **complex number** is the sum of a real number and an imaginary number. Thus, a complex number is a number of the form $a + bi$, with a and b both real numbers. Both a and b are allowed to be 0, and so any real number is also a complex number. For example, $-6 = -6 + 0i$, so -6 is a complex number.

Addition, Subtraction, and Multiplication with Complex Numbers

Addition, subtraction, and multiplication with complex numbers can all be done fairly easily by using the following rule:

Treat i just like an x, except whenever you have an i^2, replace it with -1.

By "treat i like an x", we mean that a term with a real number and a term with an i are not like terms, and must stay separate; but we can combine any two i terms the same way we combine two x terms:

$$7i - 23i = -16i$$

•Examples:

Find: 1. $(3 - 8i) + (-2 + 4i)$ 2. $(3 - 8i) - (-2 + 4i)$
      3. $(3 - 8i)(-2 + 4i)$ 4. $\left(\frac{7}{2} - 3i\right)\left(\frac{7}{2} + 3i\right)$

SOLUTION:

1. $3 - 8i + (-2) + 4i$ 2. $3 - 8i - (-2 + 4i)$
    $= (3 + (-2)) + (-8 + 4)i$ $= 3 - 8i + 2 - 4i$
    $= 1 - 4i$ $= (3 + 2) + (-8 - 4)i$
                           $= 5 - 12i$

3. Using the FOIL method, $(3 - 8i)(-2 + 4i)$:

    First terms: -6
    Outside terms: $12i$
    Inside terms: $16i$
    Last terms: $-32i^2 = (-32)(-1) = 32$
    Combining like terms: $26 + 28i$.

4. This is an example of the Difference of Squares Formula, $(a - b)(a + b) = a^2 - b^2$. Our answer is:

$$\left(\tfrac{7}{2} - 3i\right)\left(\tfrac{7}{2} + 3i\right)$$

$$= \left(\tfrac{7}{2}\right)^2 - (3i)^2$$

$$= \tfrac{49}{4} - \left(9i^2\right)$$

$$= \tfrac{49}{4} - (9)(-1)$$

$$= \tfrac{49}{4} + 9$$

$$= \tfrac{85}{4}.$$

Notice that our answer is a real number, without any i's, even though both factors had an i term.

Division of Complex Numbers

To do a complete job of dividing one complex number by another, our answer must be in the standard form of a complex number –namely, a + bi with a and b as real numbers. This method involves the the conjugate of a complex number. A **conjugate** of a complex number is defined this way:

The conjugate of a complex number a + bi is the complex number a - bi.   (The conjugate of a - bi is a + bi.)

Now the procedure for dividing one complex number by another is:

1. Express the quotient as a fraction, $\frac{a+bi}{c+di}$.

2. Multiply the top and bottom of the fraction by the conjugate of the denominator.   When simplified, this will produce a denominator which is a real number - that is, with no i term.

3. Separate the quotient into a real term and an i term.

•Example:

Divide (3 - 8i) ÷ (-2 + 4i) .

SOLUTION:

1. $\frac{3-8i}{-2+4i}$

2. $\left(\frac{3-8i}{-2+4i}\right)\left(\frac{-2-4i}{-2-4i}\right) = \frac{-38+4i}{(-2)^2-(4i)^2} = \frac{-38+4i}{20}$

3. $\frac{-38}{20} + \frac{4}{20}i = \frac{-19}{10} + \frac{1}{5}i$

We can check the answer by multiplying to get:

$$(-2 + 4i)\left(\frac{-19}{10} + \frac{1}{5}i\right) = 3 - 8i.$$

Preliminary Ideas, Exercise 4. Complex Numbers.

For each given number, specify to which sets the number belongs. Some numbers will belong to more than one set, in which case give all sets that include the number.

Integers
Rational Numbers
Real Numbers
Complex Numbers

1. $\sqrt{\frac{36}{16}}$

2. 0

3. $2 - 3i$

4. $-\frac{6}{3}$

5. $2 - \frac{3}{4}i$

6. $\sqrt{9}$

7. $\frac{2-3i}{6+2i}$

8. $\frac{5}{\sqrt{3}}$

9. -3

10. $\frac{\sqrt{100}}{\sqrt{25}}$

11. $\frac{5}{3}$

12. $2 - \sqrt{3}\,i$

13. $\sqrt{7}$

14. $\frac{3}{4}i$

15. $\frac{\sqrt{5}}{5}$

Put each number in the standard complex form of a + bi, where a and b are real numbers. Also simplify each radical as much as possible; for example, write 2 instead of $\sqrt{4}$.

16. $\sqrt{9}$

17. $\sqrt{-9}$

18. $\frac{6+\sqrt{-9}}{3}$

19. $\frac{2-\sqrt{-9}}{3}$

20. $4 - 5\sqrt{-6}$

21. $3 + \sqrt{7}$

22. $3 + \sqrt{-7}$

23. $\frac{2+\sqrt{12}}{5}$

24. $\frac{2+\sqrt{-12}}{5}$

25. $\sqrt{-72}$

Preform the indicated calculations:

26. $(2 + 7i)(-4 + 3i)$

27. $(4 - 5i)\left(-\frac{4}{5}i\right)$

28. $(-5)(-12 + 7i)$

29. $(2 + 7i) - (-4 + 3i)$

30. $\frac{5-6i}{-\frac{2}{3}+\frac{6}{7}i}$

31. $(4 - 5i) + \frac{4}{5}i$

32. $\frac{2+7i}{-4+3i}$

33. $(5 - 6i)\left(-\frac{2}{3} + \frac{6}{7}i\right)$

34. $(2 + 7i) + (-4 + 3i)$

35. $(4 - 5i) - \frac{4}{5}i$

36. $(5 - 6i) - \left(-\frac{2}{3} + \frac{6}{7}i\right)$

37. $\frac{4-5i}{\frac{4}{5}i}$

38. $\frac{-5}{-12+7i}$

39. $(5 - 6i) + \left(-\frac{2}{3} + \frac{6}{7}i\right)$

Functions

Part 1

The Idea of a Function

Functions are the building blocks of calculus and almost all mathematics beyond calculus. A **function** is a rule or formula which takes an input number, makes a calculation, and yields an output number. In this respect a function is like a computer routine which has a single input and a single output. The calculation may be very simple (for example, the function rule might be "kick out 78.3 regardless of what the input number is"), or it may be complicated.

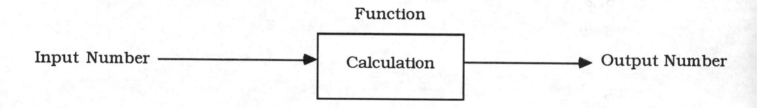

•Example:

> A familiar example of a function is the formula that converts Fahrenheit temperature to Celius:
>
> $$C = \frac{5}{9}(F - 32)$$
>
> In this case **F** stands for the input number (the Fahrenheit temperature) and **C** stands for the output number.

It is possible to have a function which does different calculations depending upon what the input number is.

•Example:

> A (comparatively simple!) income tax function might multiply the input number by .15 if the input number is less than $30,000, and multiply by .28 if the input is over $30,000.

16

HOWEVER: The one ironclad rule for functions is: If you feed in the same input number five million times, the function has to yield the same output number each time.

•Example:

> A calculation that says "multiply the input number by 7 if the time is 2:00 P.M. or earlier, otherwise add 56" is not a legal function. If you feed in the number 10, you will not get the same output number at noon as you will at 3:00 P.M.

Functional Notation

•Example:

> A function is usually defined by an equation which looks something like this:
>
> $$f(x) = 2x - 7$$
>
> In this example:
>
> > The x (on both sides) is the input number.
> > The f is the name of the function.
> > 2x - 7 is the output number
>
> Therefore, this function multiplies the input number by 2, then subtracts 7. The result is the output number. Sometimes we refer to the output number as the <u>value of f at x</u>. The left-hand side of the equation is usually read f <u>of</u> x.

Functions of a Particular Number

To find the output number from a function when a particular number is used as input, substitute the input number for "x" in the equation which defines the function.

•Example:

> If we substitute x = 3 into the equation in the example above, we get:
>
> $$f(3) = 2(3) - 7$$
> $$= 6 - 7$$
> $$= -1.$$

In words, the equation

$$f(3) = -1$$

says: If we feed the number 3 into the function f, the output number will be -1. We also say that "the value of f at 3 is -1".

Of course, the equation in the example above gives us no information at all about what happens when numbers other than 3 are used as input into f, so we use the notation with "x" when first defining a function.

Functions, Exercise 1. The Idea of a Function.

1. Let $f(x) = 5 - 3x$. Find:

    a. $f(1)$
    b. $f(0)$
    c. $f(10)$
    d. $f(\frac{5}{3})$
    e. $f(-4)$
    f. $f(-\frac{5}{3})$

2. Let $f(x) = \frac{x+3}{x-2}$. Find:

    a. $f(3)$
    b. $f(1)$
    c. $f(0)$
    d. $f(-\frac{1}{2})$

3. Let $f(x) = 2x^2 - x + 7$. Find:

    a. $f(1)$
    b. $f(2)$
    c. $f(0)$
    d. $f(\frac{2}{3})$

4. Define the functions below with functional notation:

    a. The function which adds 3 to the input number.
    b. The function which adds 3 to the input number and then multiplies the answer by itself.
    c. The function which adds 3 to the input number, and then divides the answer by 12 minus the input number.
    d. The function which raises the input number to the 5th power, then subtracts 4 times the input number, and then adds 6.
    e. The function which outputs -45 no matter what the input number is.
    f. The function which puts out the same number that comes in.

In general, all standard arithmetic operations performed with numbers can also be performed with functions. The rules work exactly as you would expect:

•Example:

Let $f(x) = x - 4$, and let $g(x) = 2x + 1$. Find:

   a. $(f + g)(x)$
   b. $(f - g)(x)$
   c. $(fg)(x)$
   d. $\left(\dfrac{f}{g}\right)(x)$

SOLUTIONS:

   a. $(f + g)(x)$
   $= f(x) + g(x)$
   $= x - 4 + 2x + 1$
   $= 3x - 3.$

   b. $(f - g)(x)$
   $= f(x) - g(x)$
   $= x - 4 - (2x + 1)$
   $= -x - 5.$

   c. $(fg)(x)$
   $= f(x)\, g(x)$
   $= (x - 4)(2x + 1)$
   $= 2x^2 - 7x - 4.$

   d. $\left(\dfrac{f}{g}\right)(x)$
   $= \dfrac{f(x)}{g(x)}$
   $= \dfrac{x-4}{2x+1}$

In each of the four parts, our answer is a new function which takes in an input number and yields an output number just like any other function.

BIG TIME WARNING:

The parentheses in $(f + g)(x)$ do NOT mean that we are multiplying!

We can also perform the same operations between a function and a number:

•Example:

> Let $f(x) = \dfrac{x+1}{x-2}$. Find:
>
> > a. $f(x) + 2$
> > b. $2 - f(x)$
> > c. $2f(x)$
> > d. $\dfrac{2}{f(x)}$
>
> SOLUTIONS:
>
> a. $f(x) + 2 = \dfrac{x+1}{x-2} + 2$　　　　b. $2 - f(x) = 2 - \dfrac{x+1}{x-2}$
>
> $\qquad\qquad = \dfrac{x+1}{x-2} + \dfrac{2(x-2)}{x-2}$　　　　$= \dfrac{2(x-2)}{x-2} - \dfrac{x+1}{x-2}$
>
> $\qquad\qquad = \dfrac{3x-3}{x-2}$　　　　　　　　　$= \dfrac{x-5}{x-2}$
>
> c. $2f(x) = 2\left(\dfrac{x+1}{x-2}\right)$　　　　d. $\dfrac{2}{f(x)} = \dfrac{2}{\frac{x+1}{x-2}}$
>
> $\qquad\quad = \dfrac{2x+2}{x-2}$　　　　　　　　$= \dfrac{2(x-2)}{x+1}$
>
> $\qquad\qquad\qquad\qquad\qquad\qquad\qquad = \dfrac{2x-4}{x+1}$

Finally, we can combine a function with algebraic expressions.

•Example:

> Let $f(x) = 6 - x$. Find:
>
> > a. $f(x) + (2x - 3)$
> > b. $(2x - 3) - f(x)$
> > c. $(2x - 3)(f(x))$
> > d. $\dfrac{f(x)}{2x-3}$
>
> SOLUTIONS:
>
> a. $f(x) + (2x - 3)$　$= 6 - x + (2x - 3)$
> $\qquad\qquad\qquad\quad = 6 - x + 2x - 3$
> $\qquad\qquad\qquad\quad = x + 3$

$$\text{b. } (2x - 3) - f(x) = (2x - 3) - (6 - x)$$
$$= 2x - 3 - 6 + x$$
$$= 3x - 9$$
$$\text{c. } (2x - 3)(f(x)) = (2x - 3)(6 - x)$$
$$= -2x^2 + 15x - 18$$
$$\text{d. } \frac{f(x)}{2x - 3} = \frac{6 - x}{2x - 3}$$

Functions, Exercise 2. Adding, Subtracting, Multiplying & Dividing Functions.

For problems 1–5, find:

a. $(f + g)(x)$
b. $(f - g)(x)$
c. $(fg)(x)$
d. $(\frac{f}{g})(x)$
e. $f(x) - 3$
f. $-2g(x)$
g. $g(x) + 3x$
h. $\frac{x+1}{f(x)}$
i. $(f + g)(1)$

1. $f(x) = x + 1$, $g(x) = x - 1$
2. $f(x) = 30x$, $g(x) = 2x$
3. $f(x) = 3$, $g(x) = x$
4. $f(x) = 2x$, $g(x) = 3x^2 + x - 19$
5. $f(x) = \frac{3x-8}{18x^5 + 3x^2 - 19x}$, $g(x) = \frac{3x-9}{18x^5 + 3x^2 - 19x}$ (parts a, b, d, f, and i only)

Part 3	**More Complicated Inputs**

For some purposes, things would be clearer if we defined functions with an empty box instead of the letter "x".

$$f (\square) = \frac{\square + 2}{2 \square - 1}$$

This is <u>exactly</u> the same as saying:

$$f(x) = \frac{x + 2}{2x - 1}$$

21

The advantage of the empty box is that we can use the following rule:

> *Whatever goes into the empty box on the left must also go into every box on the right.*

•Example:

$$f\left(\boxed{x+1}\right) = \frac{\boxed{x+1} + 2}{2\boxed{x+1} - 1}$$

This tells us that if we feed x + 1 into the function defined in the previous example, we get:

$$\frac{x+1+2}{2(x+1)-1} \qquad \text{or} \qquad \frac{x+3}{2x+1}$$

Note that the example above does NOT give us f(x) + 1!
To get f(x) + 1, we calculate:

$$f(x) + 1 = \frac{x+2}{2x-1} + 1$$
$$= \frac{x+2}{2x-1} + \frac{2x-1}{2x-1}$$
$$= \frac{3x+1}{2x-1}$$

BIG TIME WARNING

f(x+1) is decidedly NOT "f <u>times</u> x + 1"!! There is no multiplication going on here, even though you see the x + 1 in parentheses!

•Example:

Let f(x) = x^2 + 3x - 4.

    Find: a. f(2x-1)

22

b. f(2x) - 1
c. 2f(x) - 1

SOLUTIONS:

$$f\left(\boxed{}\right) = \boxed{}^2 + 3\boxed{} - 4$$

So:

a. $f\left(\boxed{2x-1}\right) = \boxed{2x-1}^2 + 3\boxed{2x-1} - 4$
$= 4x^2 - 4x + 1 + 6x - 3 - 4$
$= 4x^2 + 2x - 6$

b. $f(2x) - 1 = [(2x)^2 + 3(2x) - 4] - 1$
$= 4x^2 + 6x - 4 - 1$
$= 4x^2 + 6x - 5$

c. $2f(x) - 1 = 2(x^2 + 3x - 4) - 1$
$= (2x^2 + 6x - 8) - 1$
$= 2x^2 + 6x - 9$

Note that we get three different answers for the three parts!

Functions, Exercise 3. More Complicated Inputs.

1. Let f(x) = x - 3.
   Find: a. f(x-3)
   b. f(x) - 3
   c. $f\left(\frac{2x}{3}\right)$
   d. -3f(x)

2. Let f(x) = x^2 + 4x.
   Find: a. f(2x + 1)
   b. f(2x) + 1
   c. 2f(x) + 1
   d. f(x) + 4x

3. Let f(x) = $\frac{x^2+1}{x-2}$.
   Find: a. f(x - 2)
   b. f(x) - 2
   c. the value of f(x + 1), when x = 2.

23

4. Let f(x) = 83,299.

   Find: a. f(x + 7)

      b. f(x - 83,299)

      c. $f(\frac{x}{1000})$

      d. f(x) - 83,300

5. Let $g(x) = \frac{3x^2}{x-4}$.

   Find a. g(5) + g(2)

      b. g(5 + 2)

      c. g(x) + g(y)

      d. g(x + y)

      e. g(x - 2)

      f. g(x) - g(2)

      g. g(x) - 2

Part 4   Composition of Functions

An important way to build a new function from two already-defined functions is to use the output from one function as the input for the other function:

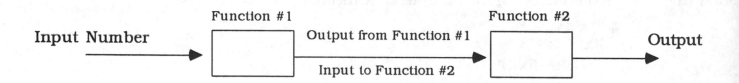

When we build a function , we say that we are *composing* the two functions, and the new function is called the **composition** or the **composite** of the two functions.

If we feed the original number x into g(x), and then feed the output of g into f(x), the resulting composite function is denoted in either of the following two ways:

    f(g(x))

    (f ∘ g)(x)   (That's a tiny circle between the f and g)

•Example:

Let f(x) = 2x - 3, and
    g(x) = 5x + 12.

Find the composite function which comes from feeding a number (x) first into g, and then using the output of g as input for f.

SOLUTION:

When we feed x into g, the number that comes out is 5x + 12. Therefore, when we feed that output number into f, we are calculating f(5x + 12) – in other words, f(g(x))! This is why the notation above makes sense. We learned how to do problems like this in the last section:

$$f(5x + 12) = 2(5x + 12) - 3$$
$$= 10x + 24 - 3$$
$$= 10x + 21.$$

Therefore, f(g(x)) = 10x + 21.

Let's check the answer in the example above by feeding the number -4 into g and then feeding the output into f. Then, let's compare the answer with what we get by feeding -4 into 10x + 21.

$$g(-4) = 5(-4) + 12$$
$$= -20 + 12$$
$$= -8$$

If we then feed -8 into f, we get:

$$f(-8) = 2(-8) - 3$$
$$= -16 - 3$$
$$= -19$$

On the other hand, if we feed -4 into the function f(g(x)) = 10x + 21, we get:

$$f(g(-4)) \quad = 10(-4) + 21$$
$$= -40 + 21$$
$$= -19.$$

Just as we predicted. To illustrate with a diagram:

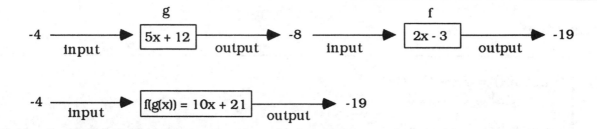

BIG TIME WARNING

It MAKES A DIFFERENCE WHICH FUNCTION COMES FIRST when you compose two functions! In the example above, g(f(x)) would be:

g(2x -3)
= 5(2x - 3) + 12
= 10x - 15 + 12
= 10x - 3.

NOT the same thing as f(g(x))!

ANOTHER BIG TIME WARNING

We can not get f(g(x)) by multiplying the two functions, or by adding them, or in any other way than using the method shown in the previous example!

•Example:

Let f(x) = -2x + 10, and
    g(x) = x + 1.

Find:
    a. f(g(x))
    b. g(f(x))
    c. (fg)(x)

26

SOLUTION:

    a. f(g(x))

        =f(x + 1)

        =-2(x + 1) + 10

        = -2x - 2 + 10

        = -2x + 8

    b. g(f(x))

        = g(-2x + 10)

        = (-2x + 10) + 1

        = -2x + 11

    c. (fg) (x)

        = (-2x + 10)(x + 1)

        = -2x^2 + 8x + 10

Note that we get three different answers!

When you get to calculus, you will find that it is to your advantage to express a complicated function as a composition of two simpler functions.

•Example:

Express $(3x^2 + 4x - 1)^{88}$ as f(g(x)), where f and g are both simpler functions than the original.

SOLUTION:

If we substitute any number for x, for instance 3, we would first substitute x = 3 into $3x^2 + 4x - 1$, and then we would raise the answer to the 88th power. That two-step procedure tells us how to solve the problem. The first function (in this case g) will be $3x^2 + 4x - 1$, and the second function (f) will be x^{88}. So our solution is:

    $(3x^2 + 4x - 1)^{88}$ = f(g(x)), where:

        $f(x) = x^{88}$, and

        $g(x) = 3x^2 + 4x - 1$.

Functions, Exercise 4. Composition of Functions.

In each problem, find:

        a. $f(g(x))$

        b. $g(f(x))$

        c. $(fg)(x)$

        d. $f(g(2))$ Find the answer in two ways: first, by substituting $x = 2$ into your answer in Part a., and second, by substituting $x = 2$ into $g(x)$ and then substituting that answer into $f(x)$.

1. $f(x) = x + 8$
   $g(x) = 8 - x$

2. $f(x) = x + 1$
   $g(x) = x + 2$

3. $f(x) = x^2 + 4$
   $g(x) = 2x$

4. $f(x) = x^{12}$
   $g(x) = x^{-3}$
   (a, b, and c only)

5. $f(x) = x^{12}$
   $g(x) = 2x - 17$
   (a, b, and c only)

6. $f(x) = \dfrac{3}{x}$
   $g(x) = x^2 + 2x - 3$

7. $f(x) = \dfrac{x+1}{x-1}$
   $g(x) = x - 1$

8. $f(x) = 3x + 5$
   $g(x) = \dfrac{x-5}{3}$

Part 5   Domains and Ranges

Domains

The **domain** of a function is the set of all numbers which can legally be used as input into the function.

•Example:

> Find the domain of the function:
>
> $$f(x) = \frac{6}{x+3}$$
>
> SOLUTION:
>
> The only input which could give us any trouble is -3, because if $x = -3$, then there is a zero in the denominator of the output number. Therefore, the domain is all real numbers except -3; or in interval notation, $(-\infty, -3) \cup (-3, \infty)$.

•Example:

Find the domain of $f(x) = \sqrt{2x - 10}$.

SOLUTION:

We are not allowed to take the square root of a negative number.
So if x is a number in the domain of f, then 2x - 10 will have to be
greater than or equal to zero. Therefore, we solve the inequality:

$$2x - 10 \geq 0$$
$$2x \geq 10$$
$$x \geq 5$$

The domain of $f(x) = \sqrt{2x - 10}$ is all numbers greater than
or equal to 5. In interval notation, the domain is $[5, \infty)$.

Sometimes a function comes with a specified domain. For example,
suppose f is the function which calculates your income tax when you input
your income from last year. The domain of the function would be all positive
numbers, because the government hasn't yet thought of taxing negative
income.

A function with a specified domain is usually written like this:

$f(x) = .23x + 500$ $\qquad\qquad (x > 1000)$

In this case, the domain of f(x) is $(1000, \infty)$.

•Example:

Find the domain of $f(x) = 5x^2 - 6x + 1$.

SOLUTION:

Any number at all can be used as input to this function, so the domain
is all real numbers.

It is worth noting that the domain of any polynomial function is all real
numbers, and the domain of a rational function is all real numbers except
those which cause the denominator to equal zero.

29

Ranges

The **range** of a function is the set of all numbers which can possibly be the output from the function. The procedure for finding the range of a given function is sometimes less clear-cut than the procedure for finding the domain, but here are some examples:

•Example:

Find the range of the function $f(x) = \sqrt{2x - 10} - 5$.

SOLUTION:

Remember that the radical sign always refers to the positive square root. Therefore $\sqrt{2x - 10}$ has to be at least zero. Since the function subtracts 5 from the square root, the output number must be at least -5. The range is therefore [-5, ∞).

•Example:

Find the range of the function $f(x) = 5 - |2x - 10|$.

SOLUTION:

The absolute value of anything is at least zero. Thus, we are subtracting at least 0 from 5 and the answer can not be greater than 5. In other words, the range is (-∞, 5].

•Example:

Find the range of the function $f(x) = \dfrac{12}{x + 7}$.

SOLUTION:

It is an important fact that a fraction can not be zero unless the numerator is zero. Since the function value is a fraction with a numerator of 12, no value of x can cause the value of the fraction to be zero. On the other hand, if you choose any number other than zero and set $\frac{12}{x+7}$ equal to the number you chose, you can solve the equation for x. That means the value you chose is in the range of f(x). The range is all numbers except zero, or $(-\infty, 0) \cup (0, \infty)$.

Functions, Exercise 5. Domains and Ranges.

Give all answers in interval notation. Find the domains of the following.

1. $f(x) = \frac{x+1}{x-1}$

2. $g(x) = \frac{x-1}{2x+10}$

3. $f(x) = \sqrt{x-3}$

4. $f(x) = \frac{1}{\sqrt{x-3}}$

5. $f(x) = \frac{x}{\sqrt{x-3}}$

6. $f(x) = x - 3$

7. $f(x) = \frac{x^2}{x}$

Find the ranges.

8. $f(x) = 2x - 1$

9. $f(x) = \sqrt{2x-1} + 3$

10. $f(x) = -|17 - x| + 4$

Part 6 Inverses

One function is an inverse of another if it 'reverses' the action of the first function. To be mathematically precise, f and g are inverses of each other if $f(g(x)) = x$ and $g(f(x)) = x$:

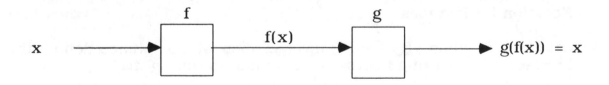

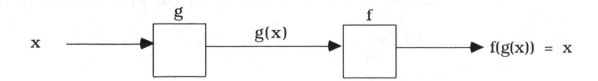

•Examples:

a. Let f(x) = x + 1, g(x) = x - 1. Then f and g are inverses because:

$$f(g(x)) = f(x - 1)$$
$$= (x - 1) + 1$$
$$= x$$
and
$$g(f(x)) = g(x + 1)$$
$$= (x + 1) - 1$$
$$= x.$$

b. Let f(x) = 3x, g(x) = $\frac{1}{3}$x. Then f and g are inverses.

c. Let f(x) = 3x + 5, and g(x) = $\frac{x - 5}{3}$, as in #8 of Exercise 4. Then f and g are inverses (the answer to both part a and part b was x).

BIG TIME WARNING

Not all functions have inverses! The absolute value function (f(x) = $|x|$), for example, has no inverse. To see this, suppose that g(x) is an inverse of f(x) = $|x|$. Then, by the definition of an inverse, g(f(3)) = 3, which means that
$$g(3) = g(|3|) = 3.$$

On the other hand, by the definition of an inverse, g(f(-3)) = -3, which means that
$$g(3) = g(|-3|) = -3.$$

But we already know that we can not possibly have g(3) equal to two different values – that's the most illegal thing a function can do!

Notation for Inverses

Let f be a function. <u>If f has an inverse</u>, then we sometimes denote the inverse of f by writing f with -1 above and to the right:

$$f^{-1}(x) = \text{inverse of } f(x)$$

This means, by definition of an inverse, that for any function f which has an inverse:

$$f(f^{-1}(x)) = x$$
$$\text{and}$$
$$f^{-1}(f(x)) = x$$

BIG TIME WARNING

The -1 'exponent' has nothing whatsoever to do with $\frac{1}{f(x)}$. The -1 isn't really an exponent. If you want to raise f(x) to the -1 power (which <u>would</u> mean $\frac{1}{f(x)}$), you would write it this way:

$$(f(x))^{-1} = \frac{1}{f(x)} \ .$$

By applying f^{-1} to both sides of the equation, f(a) = b, we get the following:

$$a = f^{-1}(f(a)) = f^{-1}(b).$$

Important Fact:

Let f be a function which has an inverse. Then, if f(a) = b, then $f^{-1}(b)$ = a.

•Example:

Suppose f is a function which has an inverse f^{-1}, and suppose that:

f(0) = 1,
f(1) = -1, and
f(2) = 2.

Find: a. $f^{-1}(1)$
     b. $f^{-1}(-1)$
     c. $f^{-1}(2)$

SOLUTION:

a. $f^{-1}(1) = f^{-1}(f(0)) = 0$

b. $f^{-1}(-1) = f^{-1}(f(1)) = 1$

c. $f^{-1}(2) = f^{-1}(f(2)) = 2$

Functions, Exercise 6.   Inverses.

1. Match each function in column A with its inverse in column B.

Column A   Column B

x $\frac{1}{2}$ x

2x $\frac{1}{2}$ (x + 7)

x + 12 $\frac{x + 2}{x - 3}$

2x - 7   x

$\frac{x - 3}{x + 2}$ x - 12

$\frac{3x + 2}{x - 1}$ $\frac{-2x - 3}{x - 1}$

2. Given: (Assume that both f and g have inverses)

f(-1) = 6
f(0) = 1
f(1) = -1
g(-1) = 3
g(3) = 1

Find: a. $f^{-1}(g(3))$
       b. $f(g^{-1}(3))$
       c. $f^{-1}(g^{-1}(3))$

The Graph of a Function

The graph of a function f(x) is the graph of the equation:

$$y = \text{(formula for f(x))}.$$

•Example:

Draw the graphs of the following functions:

1. $f(x) = 2x + 1$
2. $f(x) = x^2 - 1$
3. $f(x) = |x|$

SOLUTION:

1. This is just the graph of the equation $y = 2x + 1$, which we know is a straight line with slope 2 and y-intercept 1:

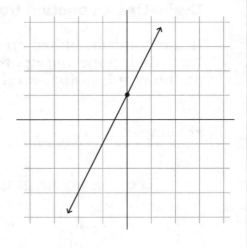

2. This is the graph of $y = x^2 - 1$, which is a parabola with vertex at (0, -1) and x-intercepts at (-1, 0) and (1, 0):

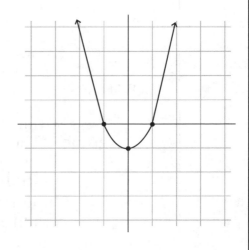

3. This is the graph of $y = |x|$, which we can draw by remembering that $|x|$ is the same as x when x is positive, and the same as -x when x is negative. So we draw the line $y = x$ to the right of the origin (where the x-coordinates are positive) and the line $y = -x$ to the left of the origin (where the x-coordinates are negative):

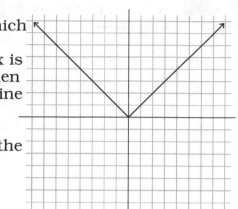

Evaluating a Function from its Graph

If the point (a, b) lies on the graph of f(x), then f(a) = b. Thus we can at least determine the approximate value of f(x) for a given value of x by looking at the graph of f(x), even if we don't know a formula for f(x).

•Example:

Looking at the graph, find:

    a. f(-2)
    b. f(0)
    c. f(3)

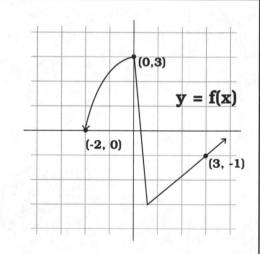

SOLUTION:

We see that the points (-2, 0), (0, 3) and (3, -1) are on the graph. Therefore:

    a. f(-2) = 0
    b. f(0) = 3
    c. f(3) = -1

Vertical Line Test

A graph is a graph of a function only if it passes the **Vertical Line Test**:

> A graph is the graph of a function if there is no vertical line which intersects the graph more than once.

•Examples:

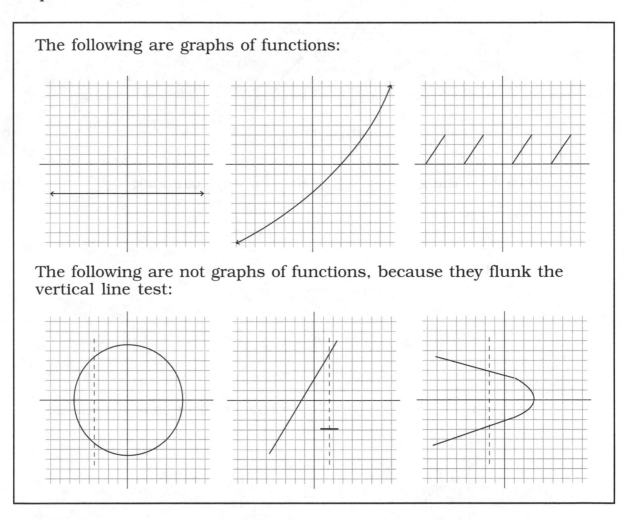

The following are graphs of functions:

The following are not graphs of functions, because they flunk the vertical line test:

Why does the Vertical Line Test work? As stated above, if a graph of f(x) contains point (a, b), that means that f(a) = b. But any two different points on the same vertical line have the same x-coordinate, but different y-coordinates. Now suppose there is a vertical line which intersects the graph of f(x) in two different points. Then we have two points; for example, (-2, 3) and (-2, 4), both on the graph of f(x). But that means f(-2) = 3 and f(-2) = 4. Once again, the most important rule for a function is that it can not give two different values for the same input number. Therefore, the graph cannot be a graph of a legitimate function.

Functions, Exercise 7. The Graph of a Function.

1. Match each function with its graph:

     a. $f(x) = -x$
     b. $f(x) = x^2$
     c. $f(x) = 4$
     d. $f(x) = 2 - |x|$

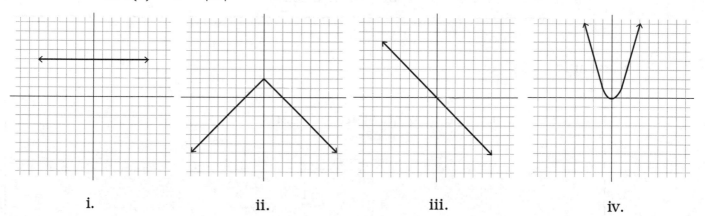

   i.   ii.   iii.   iv.

2. Based on the graph $y = f(x)$, find (or approximate):

     a. $f(-3)$
     b. $f(0)$
     c. $f(2)$
     d. $f(5)$

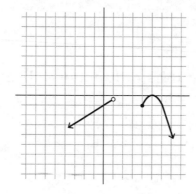

3. State which of the graphs that follow are graphs of functions:

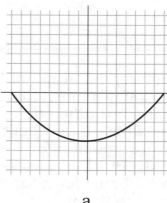 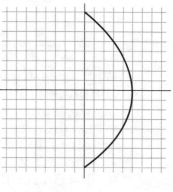

       a.   b.   c.

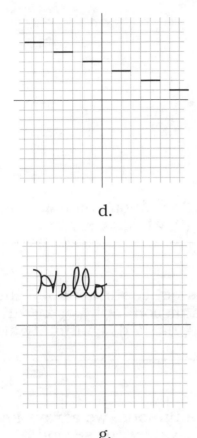

d.

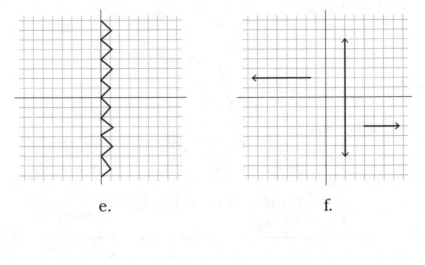

e.

f.

g.

Part 8

Continuity

A function is *continuous* if its graph has no breaks or gaps; very informally, you can draw the graph of a continuous function without lifting your pencil. We frequently say that a function is continuous *on a particular interval* if its graph has no breaks or gaps where x values are in the specified interval.

Examples:

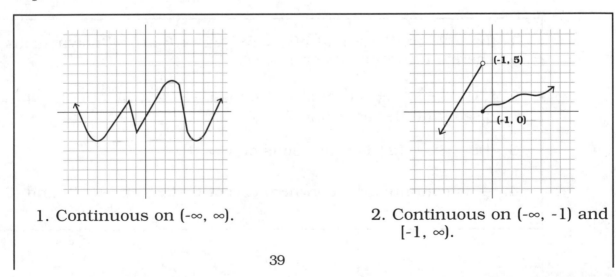

1. Continuous on (-∞, ∞).

2. Continuous on (-∞, -1) and [-1, ∞).

39

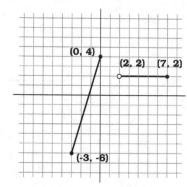

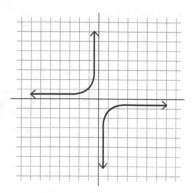

3. Continuous on [-3, 0] and (2, 7].

4. Continuous on (-∞, 0) and (0, ∞).

A *discontinuity* is a value of x where the function is not continuous. In the example above, #1 has no discontinuities: #2 has a discontinuity at x = -1; #3 has discontinuities at -3, 7, and from 0 to 2; and #4 has a discontinuity at 0.

BIG TIME WARNING

When giving the intervals on which a function is continuous, we always use the x value (going left to right on the graph). The y values, or second coordinates of the points, do not affect the continuity of the graph.

It is useful to know the following facts about continuity for various kinds of functions:

1. Polynomials are continuous everywhere (i.e.., on (-∞, ∞)).
2. Rational functions are continuous everywhere except where the denominator = 0.
3. The absolute value of any function is continuous wherever the original function is continuous.

Examples:

---

1. $f(x) = 2$, $g(x) = -x$, and $h(x) = 5x^2 - 2x + 6$ are all polynomials and therefore continuous on (-∞, ∞).

2. $f(x) = \frac{x-5}{(x+1)(x-2)}$ is continuous on (-∞, -1), (-1, 2), and (2, ∞). f has discontinuities at -1 and 2.

3. $\left| x^2 - 8x + 12 \right|$ is continuous on (-∞, ∞).

4. $\left| \frac{3}{x} \right|$ is continuous everywhere except 0 –i.e., on (-∞, 0) and (0, ∞).

Functions, Exercise 8.

In 1-4, give the interval(s) on which each function is continuous.

1.
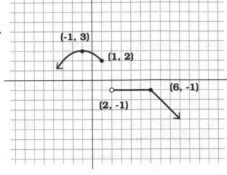

2.
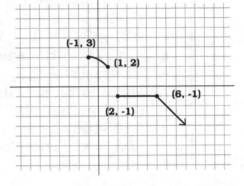

3.
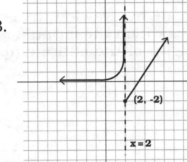

4.
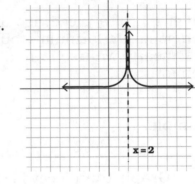

5. $f(x) = \frac{3x-4}{2}$

6. $f(x) = \left|6x^2 - 5x - 17\right|$

7. $f(x) = \frac{x-1}{x+1}$

8. $f(x) = \left|\frac{x-1}{x+1}\right|$

9. $f(x) = \left|\frac{x-2}{x^2-1}\right|$

Part 9   Piecewise Defined Functions

A *piecewise defined function* is a function which splits its domain into several intervals, using a different calculation for each interval.

Example:

Let: $f(x) = \begin{cases} 3 & x < 2 \\ 2x+1 & 2 \le x < 5 \\ x & 5 < x \end{cases}$ Find:

a. f(-6)
b. f(2)
c. f(3)
d. f(5)
e. f(7.123456789)

41

SOLUTION:

a. When the input is less than 2, f(x) = 3. -6 is less than 2, so f(-6) = 3.
b. When the input number is greater than or equal to 2, but less than
   5, f(x) = 2x + 1. Since 2 falls into the specified interval,
   f(2) = 2(2) + 1 = 5.
c. 3 falls into the same interval from 2 to 5 as we used in Part b.
   Thus, f(3) = 2(3) + 1 = 7.
d. There is no specified rule when x = 5, so 5 is not in the domain of
   this function. f(5) is undefined.
e. 7.123456789 is greater than 5. For input numbers greater than 5,
   f(x) = x. Therefore, f(7.123456789) = 7.123456789.

The graph of a piecewise defined function is made by drawing the graph for
each separate formula – but only for the x values which the formula is used.
This means we use only a piece (from left to right) of the entire graph for
each formula.

Example:

Graph the piecewise defined function from the previous example:

$$\text{Let } f(x) = \begin{cases} 3 & x < 2 \\ 2x + 1 & 2 \leq x < 5 \\ x & 5 < x \end{cases}$$

SOLUTION:

The graphs of the functions f(x) = 3, f(x) = 2x + 1, and f(x) = x
are shown separately below. On each graph are dotted vertical
lines designating the piece of the graph we will use for our
functions:

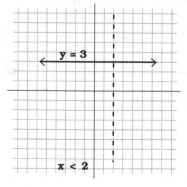 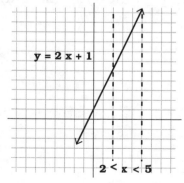 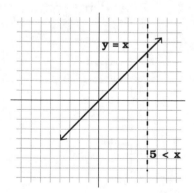

Putting all three pieces together, we get this graph:

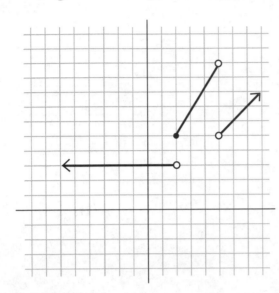

Note that we use open and closed dots just as on a number line. The open dot means that point is not included on the graph. The solid dot means the point is included.

Functions, Exercise 9. Piecewise Defined Functions.

$$\text{Let } f(x) = \begin{cases} x-1 & x < -4 \\ x^2 & -4 \leq x \leq 4 \\ 13-x & 4 < x \end{cases} \qquad g(x) = \begin{cases} 10 & x < 0 \\ x+2 & x \geq 0 \end{cases}$$

Find:
1. $f(-6)$
2. $f(-1)$
3. $f(4)$
4. $f(4.1)$
5. $g(-1)$

6. $g(0)$
7. $g(2)$
8. $f(g(2))$
9. $g(f(20))$
10. $g(g(-3))$

11. Describe $f(x) = |x|$ as a piecewise defined function.
12. Match each function with its graph on the next page.

a. $f(x) = \begin{cases} 2 & x < 1 \\ -2 & x \geq 1 \end{cases}$

b. $f(x) = \begin{cases} x & x < 3 \\ 3 - x & x \geq 3 \end{cases}$

c. $f(x) = \begin{cases} 2 & x \leq -2 \\ -2 & x > -2 \end{cases}$

d. $f(x) = \begin{cases} x & x < 1 \\ 5 & x = 1 \\ x & x > 1 \end{cases}$

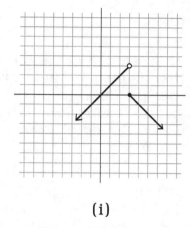

(i)

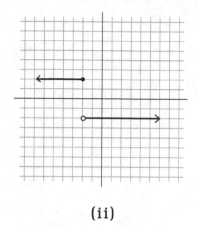

(ii)

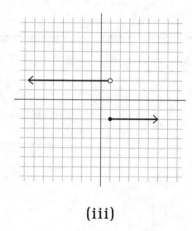

(iii)

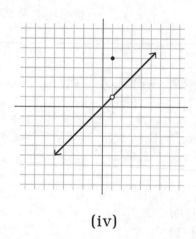

(iv)

Inequalities

An equation is a statement that two mathematical expressions have exactly equal values. An inequality is a statement that one mathematical expression has a greater value than another. We often want to know what values of x will cause a function to have a value less than 10, or greater than zero, etc. This chapter will provide some tools for answering such questions.

Part 1	Solving Inequalities from Graphs

Suppose we are given the graph of f(x), and we want to solve the inequality

$$f(x) < a.$$

If c is a number in the domain of f, then f(c) = some number d, and so the point (c,d) is on the graph of f(x). c is part of the solution to the inequality if d<a. Looking at the graph, we can tell whether d<a by checking if point (c, d) is above or below the horizontal line y = a (the graph of the equation y = a is always a horizontal line no matter what a is). If f(c)<a then the point (c, d) will be below the line y = a. From these facts we have the following procedure for solving inequalities of the form f(x)<a or f(x)>a, when given the graph of f(x):

> The solution to the inequality f(x)>a is the set of x-coordinates of all the points on the graph which lie *above* the horizontal line y = a.

> The solution to the inequality f(x)<a is the set of x-coordinates of all the points on the graph which lie *below* the horizontal line y = a.

Usually the set of points which are above (or below) the line y = a will be a collection of one or more intervals – although sometimes there may be single points.

Examples:

Solve the following inequalities:

1. f(x)>2.

2. g(x)≤0.

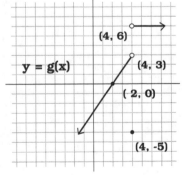

45

SOLUTIONS:

1. The graph of f(x) lies above the horizontal line y = 2 when x is between -3 and 1, and again when x is greater than 5. Therefore, the solution is (-3,1) ∪ (5,∞).

2. The graph of g(x) lies below the horizontal line y = 0 (which is the same as the x-axis) when x is less than 2, and at the single point (4, -5). Since this is a less than or equal to inequality, we must include in our solution the x-coordinates of the points where f(x) equals zero – i.e., the points where the graph intersects the line y = 0. In this case, the only such point is (2,0). Therefore, the solution is (-∞,2] ∪ {4} .

BIG TIME WARNING

The solutions to these inequalities are *always* the <u>x</u> value of the points lying above or below the line y = a. The y-coordinates of these points have nothing to do with the solution. Graphically, the solutions are intervals which go from left to right, not up and down.

Inequalities, Exercise 1. Solving Inequalities from Graphs.

Solve.

1. f(x) > 0

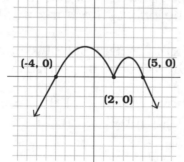

2. f(x) ≤ -2

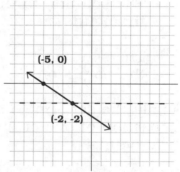

3. f(x) < 3

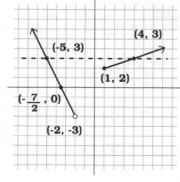

4. f(x) ≥ -3

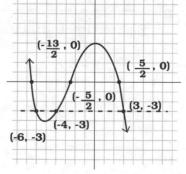

Part 2

Inequalities Involving Continuous Functions

If f(x) is a continuous function and a is any real number, then the solution to the inequality

$$f(x) < a \text{ or } f(x) > a$$

is one or more intervals whose endpoints are either plus or minus infinity, or solutions to the equation f(x) = a.

Knowing this, the procedure for solving any inequality of the form f(x) < a or f(x) > a, when f(x) is continuous everywhere, is:

1. Solve the equation f(x) = a.
2. Take all solutions from Step 1, along with plus or minus infinity, and list them in ascending order.
3. Divide a number line into intervals with endpoints from the list in Step 2.
4. For each interval in Step 3:
   - a. Choose one number from the interval (any number at all!).
   - b. Substitute the chosen number into the original inequality, and check to see whether the inequality is true.
   - c. If the inequality is true, then the interval from which the number is chosen is part of the solution.

Example:

Solve: 2x - 1 < 5.

SOLUTION:

Step 1: The only solution to 2x - 1 = 5 is x = 3.
Step 2: Our list is -∞, 3, ∞ .
Step 3: We get two intervals: (-∞, 3) and (3, ∞).
Step 4: For interval (-∞, 3):
   - a. Choose 0 (any other number from (-∞, 3) would also work).
   - b. 2(0) - 1 <u>is</u> less than 5.
   - c. So (-∞, 3) is part of the solution.

For interval (3, ∞):
   - a. Choose 5.
   - b. 2(5) - 1 is <u>not</u> less than 5.
   - c. So (3, ∞) is not part of the solution.

Conclusion: The solution is (-∞, 3).

Note that this procedure is based on what we discovered in the previous section on solving inequalities from graphs: The boundaries of the solution to the inequality f(x) < a are the points where the graph of f(x) crosses over the horizontal line y = a. And the only places where that happens are the solutions to the equation f(x) = a.

Examples:

Solve: 1. $(x - 3)(x + 4)(2x - 7)(2 - 6x) \geq 0$
2. $|x^2 - 12| < 4$.

SOLUTION:

1. $(x - 3)(x + 4)(2x - 7)(2 - 6x) = 0$ if any of the 4 individual factors = 0. So the solutions are 3, -4, $\frac{7}{2}$, and $\frac{1}{3}$. That gives us 5 intervals:

$$(-\infty,-4), \left(-4,\frac{1}{3}\right), \left(\frac{1}{3},3\right), \left(3,\frac{7}{2}\right), \text{ and } \left(\frac{7}{2},\infty\right).$$

Choosing one number from each interval and checking the inequality for each chosen number, we will find that the inequality is true for the numbers chosen from intervals $(-4,\frac{1}{3})$ and $(3,\frac{7}{2})$, but false for the numbers chosen from the other three intervals. (Note that when the other side of the inequality is zero, all we need to determine is whether each factor is positive or negative. We needn't calculate the exact value.) Therfore the solution is:

$$\left[-4,\frac{1}{3}\right] \text{ and } \left[3,\frac{7}{2}\right].$$

(We use square brackets because it's a greater than <u>or equal to</u> inequality.)

2. Using what we learned about equations involving absolute value, we set $x^2 - 12 = 4$, and $x^2 - 12 = -4$. There are 2 solutions to each equation. Using the solutions to construct intervals, we get $(-\infty, -4)$, $(-4,-\sqrt{8})$, $(-\sqrt{8},\sqrt{8})$, $(\sqrt{8},4)$, and $(4,\infty)$. We use a calculator to find that $\sqrt{8}$ is about 2.828. We can then accurately choose a number from each interval. By testing one number from each interval, we find that the solution is: $$\left(-4,-\sqrt{8}\right) \cup \left(\sqrt{8},4\right).$$

BIG TIME WARNING

You can't choose an endpoint from the interval as your number to test. It must be a number from the interior of the interval.

Inequalities, Exercise 2. Inequalities Involving Continuous Functions.

Solve each inequality.

1. $2x + 3 > 1$

2. $|2x + 3| > 1$

3. $|2x + 3| \leq 1$

4. $x^2 - 6x + 10 < 1$

5. $x^2 - 6x + 10 \leq 1$

6. $-x^2 + 5x + 1 \geq 7$

7. $(x - 5)^2 (x + 4) (2x + 17) > 0$

8. $(2x - 8) (x + 5) x \leq 0$

Part 3	**Inequalities Involving Non-continuous Functions**

An inequality of the form

$$f(x) < a \quad \text{or} \quad f(x) > a$$

when f(x) has some points of discontinuity, is solved as in the case where f(x) is continuous, but with one addition: We add the points of discontinuity to the list of possible endpoints of intervals. At this time, the only non-continuous functions with which we will work are the rational functions (fractions with one polynomial over another). Our points of discontinuity will be the values of x which cause the denominator to equal zero.

Example:

Solve the inequality $\frac{(x-1)(x+2)}{x(2x-9)} \geq 0$.

SOLUTION:

There are two solutions to the equation $\frac{(x-1)(x+2)}{x(2x-9)} = 0$; namely, 1 and -2. To find the values of x which cause the denominator to equal zero, we solve the equation $x(2x - 9) = 0$. The two solutions are 0 and $\frac{9}{2}$. Our list of possible endpoints is $-\infty$, -2, 0, 1, $\frac{9}{2}$, and ∞. That gives us five intervals to try:

$$(-\infty, -2), \ (-2, 0), \ (0, 1), \ (1, \tfrac{9}{2}), \ (\tfrac{9}{2}, \infty).$$

Just as we did in the previous section, we choose one number from each interval, substitute it into the original inequality, and see whether the inequality is true. The intervals whose chosen numbers make the inequality true are the solution. In this case, the intervals for which the inequality is true are $(-\infty, -2)$, $(0, 1)$, and $(\frac{9}{2}, \infty)$. Also, we note that this is a "greater than or equal to" inequality, and we already found that the values 1 and -2 cause the fraction to equal zero. Therefore we put a square bracket around those numbers in the solution: $(-\infty, -2] \cup (0, 1] \cup (\frac{9}{2}, \infty]$.

Inequalities, Exercise 3. Inequalities Involving Non-continuous Functions.

Solve.

1. $\dfrac{x-1}{x+1} > 0$

2. $\dfrac{|x-1|}{x+1} \geq 0$

3. $\dfrac{x^2-1}{x+4} \leq 0$

4. $\dfrac{x-2}{2x+3} \geq 1$

5. $\dfrac{x-2}{2x+3} > x$

6. $\dfrac{(x-1)(x-3)(x-5)}{(x+1)(x+3)(x+5)} < 0$

Solving Polynomial and Rational Functions for Zero

If we are trying to solve an equation, we can always subtract whatever is on the right-hand side from both sides of the equation, leaving zero on the right and some algebraic expression on the left. The left-hand side can now be thought of as a function. If we can find all values of x which cause the function on the left-hand side to equal zero, we will have solved the original equation. Therefore, the process of solving the equations is really the process of finding the values which cause functions to equal zero. This chapter will develop some methods for finding these values when the function in question is a polynomial or a rational function.

Part 1 — Division of Polynomials

If f(x) and g(x) are polynomials in the single variable x, we can divide f(x) by g(x), using the method described below. When we divide one polynomial by another, we get a quotient and a remainder, just as we do when we divide numbers. The quotient and the remainder will be polynomials. The degree of the remainder will always be strictly less than the degree of f(x). (Recall that the *degree* of a polynomial is the highest power of x occurring in the polynomial.)

When we divide f(x) by g(x), and get a quotient q(x) and a remainder r(x), the following equation is always true:

$$f(x) = g(x)\ q(x) + r(x).$$

If we divide both sides of that equation by g(x), we get:

$$\frac{f(x)}{g(x)} = q(x) + \frac{r(x)}{g(x)} \ .$$

The procedure for dividing f(x) by g(x) is similar to long division of numbers. Before beginning, write out f(x) (the dividend) with the terms in descending order of their degrees. Then fill in any "gaps" in the degrees by inserting a term with a coefficient of 0 for each missing power. For example, change

$$-3x^6 + 2x^3 - x$$
$$\text{to}$$
$$-3x^6 + 0x^5 + 0x^4 + 2x^3 + 0x^2 - x + 0 \ .$$

The details of this procedure are best explained by looking at the following example.

•Example:

Divide $f(x) = -3x^5 + 2x^4 + 23x^3 - 12x^2 - 25$
 by $g(x) = x^2 - 8.$

SOLUTION (comments to follow):

$$
\begin{array}{r}
\overset{①}{}\overset{④}{}\overset{⑦}{}\,\overset{⑩}{} \\
-3x^3 + 2x^2 - x + 4 \\
x^2 - 8 \overline{\smash{\big)}\, -3x^5 + 2x^4 + 23x^3 - 12x^2 + 0x - 25}
\end{array}
$$

② $\underline{-3x^5 + 24x^3}$

③ $2x^4 - x^3 - 12x^2$

⑤ $\underline{2x^4 - 16x^2}$

⑥ $-x^3 + 4x^2 + 0x$

⑧ $\underline{-x^3 + 8x}$

⑨ $4x^2 - 8x - 25$

⑪ $\underline{4x^2 - 32}$

⑫ $-8x + 7$

The quotient, g(x), is $-3x^3 + 2x^2 - x + 4$, and the remainder, r(x), is $-8x + 7$.

According to the formula at the beginning of this section, we can check this by seeing that:

$-3x^5 + 2x^4 + 23x^3 - 12x^2 - 25 = (x^2 - 8)(-3x^3 + 2x^2 - x + 4) + (-8x + 7).$

Comments on each step:

1. We get $-3x^3$ by dividing $-3x^5$, the first term of the dividend, by x^2, the first term of the divisor.

2. We get $-3x^5 + 24x^3$ by multiplying the $-3x^2$ on top by the entire divisor, $x^2 - 8$. We place each term of the product directly underneath the term of the same power of the dividend.

3. $2x^4 - x^3 - 12x^2$ is what we get when we subtract the polynomial in Step 2 from the corresponding terms of the dividend. Notice that we "brought down" the $-12x^2$ from the original dividend, so we would have all the terms we need to correspond with the next multiplication step (⑤). This subtraction gives us a <u>new</u> dividend, with a lower degree than the original dividend. We're making progress! We will repeat these steps until we get a dividend whose degree is <u>lower</u> than the degree of the divisor.

52

4. We get $2x^2$ by dividing x^2 into $2x^4$, the first term of the new dividend.

5. $2x^4 - 16x^2$ is the product of $2x^2$ times the divisor.

6. Subtract the polynomial ⑤ from the latest dividend, ③ . Remember that subtracting each term involves changing the sign (+ or -), and then adding. So $-12x^2 - (-16x^2) = 4x^2$.

7. We get $-x$ by dividing the first term of our latest dividend (⑥)by x^2.

8. Once again, multiplying the latest term of the quotient by the divisor.

9. Subtract ⑧ from ⑥ , as we did in Steps ③ and ⑥ .

10. We continue to divide until the degree of the latest dividend is less than the degree of divisor. In this case, the degrees are equal, so we continue. $4x^2$ divided by x^2 is 4. The 4 goes up on top.

11. Again, multiplying the latest term of the quotient by the divisor, as in Steps ② , ⑤ , and ⑧ .

12. This last polynomial has degree 1, and the divisor has degree 2. We are finished. The polynomial ⑫ is the remainder, and the polynomial on top is the quotient.

Solving Polynomial & Rational Functions for Zero, Exercise 1.
Division of Polynomials.

Perform each division and find the quotient f(x) and the remainder r(x):

1. $(x^5 - 8x^3 + 3x^2 + x - 23) \div (x^2 - 8)$ 2. $(3x^5 - 5x^4 + 2x - 4) \div (x^3 + 2)$

3. $(x^3 + 64) \div (x + 1)$ 4. $(x^6 + x^5 + x^4 + 2x^3 + 2x - 3) \div (x^3 + 1)$

5. $(4x^4 - 2x^3 + x^2 - 1) \div (x^2 - 2)$ 6. $(x^4 + 9x^2 + 20) \div (x^2 + 4)$

7. $(1 - x^4) \div (x^2 + 1)$ 8. $(x^4 + x^2 + 2) \div (x^2 + x + 1)$

9. $(10x^3 + 8x^2 + 25x + 20) \div (2x^2 + 5)$ 10. $(x^4 - 81) \div (x + 3)$

11. $(4x^4 + 5x - 6) \div (4x - 3)$ 12. $(5x^7 - 3x^4 + 2x^2 - 3) \div (2x^2 - x + 1)$

13. $(25x + 28x^3 - 9 - 47x^2 - 12x^4) \div (6x^2 - 5x + 4)$

14. $(3x^2 - 2x - 1) \div (6x^5 + 4x^4 - 3x^2 + x - 2)$

15. $(9x^2 + 7x + 5x^5 - 3x^3 - 15x^4 - 21) \div (x - 3)$

53

Synthetic Division

If you have a polynomial division problem in which the divisor is simply x plus or minus some number, there is a quicker method of division. It is called **synthetic division**. It is shown below.

We begin the process by writing the dividend, in descending order of degrees, filling in with zeros where there is a missing term, just as we did with long division. The difference this time is that we will write only the <u>coefficients</u> of the terms, not the x's and exponents. Where we used to write the divisor, we write only the constant (number alone) term of the divisor, with the *sign changed*. For example, if we are dividing by x - 8, we write the number 8. If we are dividing by x + 5, we write -5. The rest of the procedure is best illustrated with an example.

•Example:

Divide $2x^4 - 8x^3 + 9x - 30$ by x - 3.

SOLUTION:

$$
\begin{array}{r|rrrrr}
3 & 2 & -8 & 0 & 9 & -30 \\
  &   & \text{(b.)} & \text{(d.)} & \text{(f.)} & \text{(h.)} \\
  &   & 6 & -6 & -18 & -27 \\
\hline
  & \text{(a)} & \text{(c.)} & \text{(e.)} & \text{(g.)} & \text{(i.)} \\
  & 2 & -2 & -6 & -9 & -57
\end{array}
$$

<u>Comments</u>:

a. The first step is to bring down the first coefficient in the dividend, in this case 2.

b. We now multiply the 2 from Step a by the divisor 3, and write the answer (6) directly below the next dividend coefficient to the right.

c. We get the -2 by *adding* the two numbers -8 and 6. <u>We do not subtract, as we do in long division.</u>

d. Multiply the -2 from Step c by 3, and write the answer in the next column to the right, just as in Step b.

e. Again we add the two numbers in the column; in this case the sum is -6.

f. The product -6 times 3 is written in the next column.

g. Add the two numbers in the column again.

h. -9 times 3.

i. Add the two numbers, as before.

j. Here's the punch line: The last number on the right is the remainder and the numbers in the bottom row before the last one are the coefficients of the quotient. (Really!) We can figure out which power of x goes with which coefficient by starting with the rightmost coefficient, which will be the constant term (number standing alone), and increasing the power of x by one for each coefficient to the left.

So, in this case, the quotient q(x) is

$$2x^3 - 2x^2 - 6x - 9$$

and the remainder is -57. Using the formula from the previous section, this tells us that

$$2x^4 - 8x^3 + 9x - 30 = (x - 3)(2x^3 - 2x^2 - 6x - 9) - 57.$$

BIG TIME WARNINGS

1. Synthetic division can be used <u>only</u> when the divisor has the form x + c or x - c for some number c. It simply doesn't work for any other division problems.

2. If we are dividing by x + c, we put -c to the left of the division box. If we are dividing by x - c, we put a *positive* c to the left of the box.

3. When we do the work on the lines below the box, we *add* the columns instead of subtracting them as we do in long division.

One further example, without any distracting comments:

•Example:

Divide $3x^5 + 2x^4 - 3x^3 + 4x^2 - 5x + 14$ by x + 2.

SOLUTION:

$$
\begin{array}{r|rrrrrr}
-2 & 3 & 2 & -3 & 4 & -5 & 14 \\
   &   & -6 & 8 & -10 & 12 & -14 \\
\hline
   & 3 & -4 & 5 & -6 & 7 & 0
\end{array}
$$

So the quotient is $3x^4 - 4x^3 + 5x^2 - 6x + 7$, with a remainder of <u>zero</u>. That means that the dividend factors evenly:

$$3x^5 + 2x^4 - 3x^3 + 4x^2 - 5x + 14 = (x + 2)(3x^4 - 4x^3 + 5x^2 - 6x + 7)$$

The Remainder Theorem

It is a remarkable fact that if $f(x)$ is a polynomial function, and c is any number at all, we can find $f(c)$ by dividing $f(x)$ by $x - c$, and then taking the remainder. Problems like this are made to order for synthetic division.

•Example:

Let $f(x) = 3x^4 - 295x^3 - 203x^2 + 494x + 50$. Find $f(99)$.

SOLUTION: We divide $f(x)$ by $x - 99$, which means we put a *positive* 99 in the position of the divisor – i.e., the "divisor" will always be the number we are plugging into the function, *not* the negative of the number.

```
99 | 3   -295   -203    494    50
   |      297    198   -495   -99
   | 3      2     -5     -1   (-49)
```

So $f(99) = -49$. (Consider how complicated it would be to calculate $f(99)$ directly.)

Solving Polynomials and Rational Functions for Zero, Exercise 2. Synthetic Division and the Remainder Theorem.

In problems 1-9, perform the indicated synthetic division and find the quotient, $q(x)$, and the remainder, r.

1. $(4x^6 + 8x^5 - 4x^4 - 5x^3 + 3x^2 - 3x + 2) \div (x - 2)$

2. $(4x^6 + 8x^5 - 4x^4 - 5x^3 + 3x^2 - 3x + 2) \div (x + 2)$

3. $(x^4 + 3x^3 - 9x^2 + 4x) \div (x - 3)$

4. $(6x^3 - 4x^2 + 3x + 2) \div (x + \frac{1}{2})$

5. $(2x^5 + 2x^3 - 4x^2 + 7) \div (x + 3)$

6. $(x^4 - 3x^2 + 2x) \div (x + 2)$

7. $(3x^4 + 16x^3 - 23x^2 + 82x - 11) \div (x + 7)$

8. $(7x^4 - 17x^3 - 11x^2 - 6x + 5) \div (x - 3)$

9. $(x^4 - 101x^3 + 201x^2 - 295x - 197) \div (x - 99)$

In problems 10-18, use synthetic division to find the indicated function value for the given function.

10. $f(x) = 2x^5 - 2x^3 - 6x^2 + 6$; $f(5)$

11. $f(x) = 2x^5 - 2x^3 - 6x^2 + 6$; $f(-5)$

12. $g(x) = 2x^4 - 3x^3 + x$; $g(2)$

13. $f(x) = 2x^5 + 3x^4 - 6x^3 - x^2 + 16x + 1$; $f(-2)$

14. $k(x) = 20x^4 - 100x^3 + x^2 - 11x + 28$; $k(5)$

15. $f(x) = 19x^4 + 96x^3 + 4x^2 - 7x - 23$; $f(-5)$

16. $f(x) = x^7 - 4x^6 - 9x + 47$; $f(4)$

17. $f(x)$ $x^5 + 3x^4 + 5x^3 + 7x^2 + 9x + 5$; $f(-1)$

18. $f(x) = x^5 + 3x^4 + 5x^3 + 7x^2 + 9x + 5$; $f(1)$

| Part 3 | **The Rational Zeros Theorem** |

A number r for which f(r) = 0 is called a **root**, or a **zero**, of the function f.

An immediate consequence of the Remainder Thoerem in the previous section is the following:

Factor Theorem

> The number c is a zero of the polynomial function p(x) if and only if (x - c) is a factor of p(x). In other words, if p(x) can be factored into (x - c) times some other factors.

Before describing a method for finding the zeros of a polynomial function, let us recall that an *integer* is a whole number - positive, negative, or zero; and that a *rational number* is a number which can be expressed as a fraction with an integer on top and an integer on the bottom. Integers themselves are rational numbers (given any integer, we can just put it on the top of a fraction and then put the integer "1" on the bottom).

Rational Zeros Theorem

> Suppose f(x) is a polynomial function whose coefficients are all integers. Let a = the coefficient of the highest power of x, and let c = the constant term of the polynomial (the number with no "x"). Then the only possibilities for rational zeros of f(x) are the positive or negative numbers $\pm \frac{r}{s}$ such that r is a divisor of c, and s is a divisor of a.

Let $f(x) = 3x^3 + 4x^2 + 6x + 8$. Then, using the terminology above, we have a = 3 and c = 8. The divisors of 3 are 1 and 3. The divisors of 8 are 1, 2, 4, and 8. If we take all possible fractions where the numerator ("r") is a divisor of 8 and the denominator ("s") is a divisor of 3, we get the following list:

$$\pm\left(\frac{1}{1}, \frac{2}{1}, \frac{4}{1}, \frac{8}{1}, \frac{1}{3}, \frac{2}{3}, \frac{4}{3}, \frac{8}{3}\right)$$

The plus or minus indicates that both the positive and the negative version of each number are possible candidates for zeros of f.

BIG TIME WARNINGS

1. The list of "candidate zeros" we get by using the Rational Zeros Theorem is just a list of *possible* zeros. It is perfectly possible that no number on the list is actually a zero of f. What we *can* say, however, is that any rational number which is *not* on the list cannot possibly be a zero of f.

2. The list of candidate zeros is only the list of possible *rational* zeros. The list does not include irrational numbers, such as $\sqrt{2}$. So an equation like $x^2 - 2$, with zeros that are plus and minus $\sqrt{2}$, will have none of its zeros on the list.

By combining the Rational Zero Theorem with other facts we know, we can often find all the zeros of a polynomial. Two additional facts we will need are the following:

1. The number of zeros of any polynomial is less than or equal to the degree of the polynomial (for example, if we have already found four zeros of a polynomial which has a degree of four, then we know we've found them all).

2. If we factor a polynomial into two or more factors, then any zero of the entire polynomial must be a zero of one of the factors.

•Example:

Find all zeros of the function $f(x) = 5x^3 + 7x^2 - 31x + 15$.

SOLUTION:

First we make a list of all numerators and denominators
of possible rational zeros:

numerators (divisors of 15): 1, 3, 5, 15
denominators (divisors of 5): 1, 5.

Putting the lists together, the possible rational zeros are:

$$\pm\left(\frac{1}{1}, \frac{3}{1}, \frac{5}{1}, \frac{15}{1}, \frac{1}{5}, \frac{3}{5}, \frac{5}{5}, \frac{15}{5}\right)$$

By the way, notice that we can eliminate $\frac{5}{5}$ and $\frac{15}{5}$ from our list, since they are equal to numbers listed earlier (1 in the case of $\frac{5}{5}$, and 3 in the case of $\frac{15}{5}$). For each number on the list, we can do synthetic division to find out whether it is a zero of f(x). This might be tedious, but it is better than trying every number in the world! We show just two examples: 3, which does not work, and $\frac{3}{5}$, which does:

$$
\begin{array}{r|rrrr}
3 & 5 & 7 & -31 & 15 \\
  &   & 15 & 66 & 105 \\
\hline
  & 5 & 22 & 35 & \boxed{120}
\end{array}
$$

$$
\begin{array}{r|rrrr}
\frac{3}{5} & 5 & 7 & -31 & 15 \\
  &   & 3 & 6 & -15 \\
\hline
  & 5 & 10 & -25 & \boxed{0}
\end{array}
$$

Our synthetic division not only shows that $\frac{3}{5}$ is a zero of f(x), it also shows that f(x) factors into $(x - \frac{3}{5})(5x^2 + 10x - 25)$. So now we can find the zeros by setting each factor separately equal to zero:

$x - \frac{3}{5} = 0$, so $x = \frac{3}{5}$ is a solution (we knew that already),
$5x^2 + 10 - 25 = 0$: this one we can solve by using the quadratic formula*, with a = 5, b = 10, and c = -25:

$$x = \frac{-10 \pm \sqrt{100 - 4(5)(-25)}}{10} = \frac{-10 \pm \sqrt{600}}{10}$$

$$= \frac{-10 \pm 10\sqrt{6}}{10} = -1 \pm \sqrt{6}$$

Now we have found three zeros of f(x): $\frac{3}{5}, -1 + \sqrt{6}$, and $-1 - \sqrt{6}$.

Since f(x) has degree = 3, we know we've found them all.

59

> *Remember that the quadratic formula says that the solutions to $ax^2 + bx + c = 0$ are $\dfrac{-b \pm \sqrt{b^2 - 4ac}}{2a}$.

Thus our procedure for finding the zeros of a polynomial with integer coefficients is:

1. Make one list of all constant term divisors, and another list of all divisors of the coefficient of the highest power of x.

2. Make a list of the candidates for rational zeros, by taking all possible combinations of the two lists from Step 1. Remember to consider both plus and minus for each candidate.

3. Use synthetic division to test each candidate zero.

4. Suppose we find a candidate which 'works' (i.e., the remainder is zero when we do the synthetic division). Then, if the successful candidate was c, we can factor the original polynomial into (x - c) times the quotient polynomial, q(x). q(x) will have a lower degree than the original polynomial.

5. We repeat Steps 1 through 4 for q(x). We keep repeating the process until the remaining quotient has degree 2. Once we are down to degree = 2, we have a quadratic which we can solve by factoring, or, if necessary, by the quadratic formula.

•A More Complicated Example:

Find the zeros of: $f(x) = \frac{1}{3}x^5 - \frac{4}{3}x^4 + \frac{4}{3}x^3 + 9x^2 - 36x + 36$.

SOLUTION:

We can't begin by writing the divisors of 36 and $\frac{1}{3}$, because all the coefficients aren't integers. But we can multiply the polynomial by 3, and get a new polynomial whose coefficients are integers. Any zero of f(x) will also be a zero of 3f(x), so we are within our rights to multiply by 3. Now we are looking for the zeros of:

$$3f(x) = x^5 - 4x^4 + 4x^3 + 27x^2 - 108x + 108 .$$

The divisors of 108 are 1, 2, 3, 4, 6, 9, 12, 18, 27, 36, 54, and 108. The only divisor of 1 is 1 itself.

As in the previous example, we show only one sample candidate which

---

doesn't work, and one which does:

$$
\begin{array}{r|rrrrr}
1 & 1 & -4 & 4 & 27 & -108 & 108 \\
  &   & 1 & -3 & 1 & 28 & -80 \\
\hline
  & 1 & -3 & 1 & 28 & -80 & \boxed{28} \\
\end{array}
$$

$$
\begin{array}{r|rrrrr}
2 & 1 & -4 & 4 & 27 & -108 & 108 \\
  &   & 2 & -4 & 0 & 54 & -108 \\
\hline
  & 1 & -2 & 0 & 27 & -54 & \boxed{0} \\
\end{array}
$$

So now we know that f(x) factors as:

$$f(x) = (x - 2)(x^4 - 2x^3 + 27x - 54)$$

The candidate zeros for $x^4 - 2x^3 + 27x - 54$ are:

$$\pm(1,2,3,6,9,18,27,54)$$

Since we have already tried 1 and it did not work, we won't try it again. But we have to try 2 again:

$$
\begin{array}{r|rrrr}
2 & 1 & -2 & 0 & 27 & -54 \\
  &   & 2 & 0 & 0 & 54 \\
\hline
  & 1 & 0 & 0 & 27 & \boxed{0} \\
\end{array}
$$

Now we know that $x^4 - 2x^3 + 27x - 54 = (x - 2)(x^3 + 27)$, which means that our original function factors as:

$$(x - 2)(x - 2)(x^3 + 27)$$

The divisors of 27 are 1, 3, 9, and 27. Once again, we already know that 1 won't work, so we don't try it. We do have to try -1, however. Below are our tests of -1 and -3.

$$
\begin{array}{r|rrr}
-1 & 1 & 0 & 0 & 27 \\
   &   & -1 & 1 & -1 \\
\hline
   & 1 & -1 & 1 & \boxed{26} \\
\end{array}
$$

$$
\begin{array}{r|rrr}
-3 & 1 & 0 & 0 & 27 \\
   &   & -3 & 9 & -27 \\
\hline
   & 1 & -3 & 9 & \boxed{0} \\
\end{array}
$$

Now we can factor f(x) as: $(x - 2)(x - 2)(x + 3)(x^2 - 3x + 9)$.

By using the quadratic formula with a = 1, b = -3, and c = 9, we find that x^2 - 3x + 9 has no real zeros. Therefore the only real zeros of $\frac{1}{3}x^5 - \frac{4}{3}x^4 + \frac{4}{3}x^3 + 9x^2 - 36x + 36$ are 2 and - 3.

Solving Polynomials and Rational Functions for Zero, Exercise 3. The Rational Zero Theorem.

Find all real zeros for each function.

1. x^5 - $2x^4$ - $18x^3$ - $32x^2$ - 23x - 6

2. x^3 + $3x^2$ - 7x - 21

3. $2x^3$ + x^2 - 3x + 1

4. x^5 - $15x^4$ + $90x^3$ - $270x^2$ + 405x - 243

5. x^3 + $6x^2$ + 11x + 6

6. x^3 - $5x^2$ + 4x - 20

7. $3x^3$ + $13x^2$ + 20x - 20

8. $\frac{1}{3}x^3 - x + \frac{2}{3}$

9. x^4 - $24x^2$ - 25

10. x^4 - $2x^3$ + $4x^2$ + 3x + 6

11. $3x^5$ + $5x^4$ - $10x^3$ - $9x^2$ + 13x -2

12. $2x^3$ - 78x - 140

Part 4 Complex Zeros

So far, when talking about the zeros of a polynomial, we have been talking about *real* zeros. But if we allow complex numbers into the domain of a polynomial function, we will sometimes find that the polynomial has one or more zeros which are not real numbers, but rather complex numbers. Remember that a *complex number* is a number of the form a + bi where a and b are both real numbers.

•Examples:

The only zeros of x^2 + 9 are $\sqrt{-9}$ and $-\sqrt{-9}$, which are 3i and -3i.

If we use the quadratic formula to find the zeros of x^2 + 2x + 5, we get two solutions:

$$\frac{-2+\sqrt{-16}}{2} \text{ and } \frac{-2-\sqrt{-16}}{2}, \text{ which are -1 + 2}i \text{ and -1 -2}i.$$

If we include complex numbers as allowable zeros, we have a theorem so important that it is called the:

Fundamental Theorem of Algebra:

Every polynomial of degree greater than zero has at least one zero in the complex numbers.

The examples above show that the Fundamental Theorem of Algebra is not true if we allow only real zeros: $x^2 + 9$ has no real zeros.

BIG TIME WARNING

The Fundamental Theorem of Algebra does not guarantee that we can <u>find</u> the zeros of any polynomial. It just says that the zeros exist somewhere in the set of of complex numbers.

Once we allow complex numbers as zeros of polynomials, we can find zeros using the same method we used in the previous section, with one addition: When we get our polynomial down to a quadratic, we will include the solutions we get from the quadratic formula, even if there is a negative under the radical.

•Example:

Find the zeros of $\frac{1}{3}x^5 - \frac{4}{3}x^4 + \frac{4}{3}x^3 + 9x^2 - 36x + 36$.

This is the last polynomial example in Part 3 (The Rational Zero Theorem) for which we found zeros.. When we used the quadratic formula on the polynomial $x^2 - 3x + 9$, we said there were no real zeros. However, if we bring complex numbers into the picture, we can see that the zeros of $x^2 - 3x + 9$ are:

$$\frac{3+\sqrt{-27}}{2} \text{ and } \frac{3-\sqrt{-27}}{2}, \text{ or } \frac{3}{2}+\frac{3\sqrt{3}}{2}i \text{ and } \frac{3}{2}-\frac{3\sqrt{3}}{2}i .$$

Therefore, the complete set of complex zeros for the original polynomial, $\frac{1}{3}x^5 - \frac{4}{3}x^4 + \frac{4}{3}x^3 + 9x^2 - 36x + 36$, is

$$2, -3, \frac{3}{2}+\frac{3\sqrt{3}}{2}i, \text{and } \frac{3}{2}-\frac{3\sqrt{3}}{2}i .$$

Solving Polynomials and Rational Functions for Zero, Exercise 4. Complex Zeros.

Find all complex zeros of each function.

1. $x^4 + x^2 - 2$

2. $5x^3 + 33x^2 - 12x + 14$

3. $x^3 - 3x^2 + 9x + 13$

4. $x^3 - 4x^2 + 21x - 34$

5. $2x^4 - 5x^3 + 15x^2 - 45x - 27$

6. $5x^4 - 4x^3 - 25x^2 + 80x - 48$

7. $x^4 - 6x^3 - 59x^2 + 294x + 490$

8. $5x^3 + 7x^2 + 40x + 56$

9. $x^4 + 4x^3 - 7x^2 - 22x + 24$

10. $6x^4 + 7x^3 + 12x^2 + x - 2$

Complete Factorization of Polynomials

The Factor Theorem tells us that if c is a zero of the polynomial p(x), then (x - c) is a factor of p(x). It is possible that (x - c) might occur more than once in the factorization of p(x). For example, if we completely factor the polynomial $p(x) = x^4 + 5x^3 + 6x^2 - 4x - 8$, we get (x + 2) (x + 2) (x + 2) (x - 1) – or, more conveniently, $(x + 2)^3$ (x - 1). Since (x + 2) is a factor of p(x), we know that -2 is a zero of p(x). Also, since (x + 2) occurs <u>three times</u> in the factorization of p(x), we say that -2 is a zero <u>of multiplicity 3</u> of p(x).

Formally:

> If c is a zero of the polynomial p(x), then the <u>multiplicity</u> of c is the number of times the factor (x - c) occurs in the complete factorization of p(x).

Now we have a theorem which summarizes our knowledge of the relationship between factoring a polynomial and finding zeros of the polynomial:

Let:
    p(x) be a polynomial.
    a = the coefficient of the highest power of x.
    d = the degree of p(x).

Then:
1. p(x) has <u>exactly</u> d complex zeros, if we count each zero as many times as its multiplicity.
2. p(x) can be factored as (a)(x - c_1) (x - c_2).....(x - c_d) where there are exactly d factors of the form (x - c_i) and the c's are all the zeros (*including* complex zeros) of p(x.)

BIG TIME WARNING

When the theorem says p(x) "can be" factored, it doesn't mean that any human being, or even a computer, can actually do the factoring. It just means the factors exist somewhere in the complex number system.

Find a polynomial whose zeros are:

a. 2, - 3, 6 + 2i, and 6 - 2i.
b. 4 and -3, with a multiplicity of 4 for -3.
c. 1 with a multiplicity of 2, and -2. Furthermore, construct the polynomial so that f(2) = 6.

SOLUTIONS:

a. $(x - 2) (x + 3) (x - (6 + 2i)) (x - (6 - 2i))$.
   If we multiply it all out (which is not necessary), we get
   $x^4 - 11x^3 + 22x^2 + 112x - 240$.
b. $(x - 4) (x + 3)^4$.
c. To get the zeros we want, we start with $(x - 1)^2 (x + 2)$. But if we leave it that way, we will find that f(2) = 4. However, we can multiply the polynomial by $\frac{3}{2}$, which will cause f(2) to = 6. So our answer is $\frac{3}{2}(x - 1)^2 (x + 2)$.

•Example:

Factor $p(x) = 3x^5 + 11x^4 + 2x^3 + 34x^2 + 123x - 45$ completely.

SOLUTION:

Our theorems tell us that this problem is equivalent to finding all the zeros of p(x), along with the multiplicity of each. We first try to find rational zeros. By our Rational Zeros Theorem, the candidates for rational zeros are: $\pm\left(1, 3, 5, 9, 15, 45, \frac{1}{3}, \frac{5}{3}\right)$

We will show the synthetic division only for the successful candidates.

-3	3	11	2	34	123	-45
		- 9	-6	12	-138	45
	3	2	-4	46	- 15	0

So now $p(x) = (x + 3) (3x^4 + 2x^3 - 4x^2 + 46x - 15)$

$$\begin{array}{r|rrrrr}
-3 & 3 & 2 & -4 & 46 & -15 \\
 & & -9 & 21 & -51 & 15 \\
\hline
 & 3 & -7 & 17 & -5 & 0
\end{array}$$

And now p(x) = (x + 3) (x + 3) ($3x^3$ - $7x^2$ + 17x - 5), or
(x + 3)^2 ($3x^3$ - $7x^2$ + 17x - 5).

$$\begin{array}{r|rrrr}
\frac{1}{3} & 3 & -7 & 17 & -5 \\
 & & 1 & -2 & 5 \\
\hline
 & 3 & -6 & 15 & 0
\end{array}$$

Now we have $p(x) = (x+3)^2\left(x-\frac{1}{3}\right)\left(3x^2-6x+15\right)$. All we have to do now is solve the quadratic equation:

$$3x^2 - 6x + 15 = 0$$

According to the quadratic formula, the solutions are:

$$x = \frac{6\pm\sqrt{36-4(15)(3)}}{6} = \frac{6\pm\sqrt{-144}}{6} = \frac{6\pm12i}{6}$$

$$=1 \pm 2i, \text{ or } 1 + 2i \text{ and } 1 - 2i.$$

Factor out 3 – the coefficient of the original highest power term – and our answer is:

$$p(x) = 3(x+3)^2\left(x-\frac{1}{3}\right)\left(x-(1+2i)\right).\left(x-(1-2i)\right)$$

Solving Polynomials and Rational Functions for Zero, Exercise 5. Complete Factorization of Polynomials.

In problems 1-8, form the polynomial p(x) which fits the requirements. Leave the answer in factored form.

1. p(x) has zeros of 3 and -13

2. p(x) has zeros of 3 with multiplicity 6, and -13

3. p(x) has zeros of 3 and -13, and p(4)=-34

4. p(x) has zeros of 0, -1, and 2

5. p(x) has zeros of 0 with multiplicity 3, -1, and 2

6. p(x) has zeros of 0 with multiplicity 3, -1, and 2, and p(1)=-1

7. p(x) has zeros of 2, -3, i, and 6 - i

8. p(x) has zeros of i with multiplicity 2, 2 with multiplicity 3, -3, and 6 - i

In problems 9-16, form the polynomial p(x) which fits the requirements. Multiply the polynomial out; do not leave it factored.

9. p(x) has zeros of -1 and 2

10. p(x) has zeros of -1, 2, and -3

11. p(x) has zeros of -1, 2, and -3, and p(0)=2

12. p(x) has zeros of 2, 3+i, and 3-i

13. p(x) has zeros of 2 with multiplicity 2, 3+i, and 3-i

14. p(x) has zeros of 0 with multiplicity 6, 4+5i, and 4-5i

15. p(x) has zeros of 0 with multiplicity 6, 4+5i, and 4-5i, and p(-1)= 25

16. p(x) has zeros of i, -i, 2+6i, and 2-6i

In problems 17-22, factor the polynomial completely.

17. $x^4 - 2x^3 + 2x^2 - 2x + 1$

18. $x^4 - 2x^3 - 4x^2 + 18x - 45$

19. $6x^3 - 9x^2 - 9x + 6$

20. $x^4 + 8x^3 + 24x^2 + 32x + 16$

21. $\frac{1}{3}x^3 - 3x^2 + 9x - 9$

22. $3x^4 - 27x^3 + 159x^2 - 483x + 348$

Part 6	**Zeros of Rational Functions**

The zeros of a rational function are the same as the zeros of the <u>numerator</u>, EXCEPT those which are also zeros of the denominator.

Using this fact, we can find the zeros of any rational function by using the same methods as in the previous sections.

•Examples:

a. Find the zeros of $f(x) = \frac{2x^3+3x^2-29x+30}{x+1}$

b. Find the zeros of $f(x) = \frac{2x^3+3x^2-29x+30}{x^2-x-2}$

SOLUTION:

a. Using methods we have already discussed, we find that the zeros of the numerator $2x^3 + 3x^2 - 29x + 30$ are 2, -5, and $\frac{3}{2}$. None of those numbers are zeros of the denominator. Therefore the zeros of the original rational function are 2, -5, and $\frac{3}{2}$.

b. We have the same numerator we had in Part (a), but this time 2 is also a zero of the denominator. Therefore 2 is not a zero of the function, because 2 is not even in the domain of the function. The zeros of the function are -5 and $\frac{3}{2}$. Note that if we factor and reduce this function, we get:

$$\frac{2x^3+3x^2-29x+30}{x^2-x-2} = \frac{(x-2)(x+5)(2x-3)}{(x-2)(x+1)} = \frac{(x+5)(2x-3)}{x+1}$$

However, the two functions are not exactly the same, because 2 is not in the domain of the original function, but 2 is in the domain of the reduced function.

Solving Polynomials and Rational Functions for Zero, Exercise 6. Zeros of Rational Functions.

Find all zeros .

1. $\frac{x+1}{x-1}$

2. $\frac{x-2}{x^2-x-2}$

3. $\frac{x^2+x-2}{x+2}$

4. $\frac{x^3-5x^2+8x-6}{x^2+2x+2}$

5. $\frac{x^3-5x^2+8x-6}{x^2-2x+2}$

6. $\frac{x^4-12x^3+54x^2-108x+81}{x^2-9}$

7. $\frac{x^5-12x^4+54x^3-108x^2+81x}{x^2-9}$

8. $\frac{x^2-9}{x^5-12x^4+54x^3-108x^2+81x}$

9. $\frac{2x^2-x-3}{-2x^2-5x+12}$

10. $\frac{2x^2-x-3}{-2x^2-5x+13}$

Part 7   Summary

Suppose p(x) is a polynomial, written with the powers of x in descending order, and with the constant term last. Let:

a = the coefficient of the first term of p(x)
d = the degree of p(x)
k = the last (constant) term of p(x).

Then, collecting the important facts about finding the zeros of rational and polynomial functions:

1. If c is any (complex) number, then the following statements are all equivalent (if any one of them is true, then they are all true):
   a. c is a zero of p(x).
   b. (x - c) is a factor of p(x).

c. If we divide p(x) by (x - c), we get a remainder of zero.
d. If we perform synthetic division on the coefficients of p(x), with a divisor of c (not negative c), the last number at the lower right will be 0.

2. Counting multiplicities, p(x) has exactly d (complex) zeros.

3. We 'can' factor p(x) into 'a', times factors of the form (x - c). There will be exactly d factors of the form (x - c), and the c's will be all the (complex) zeros of p(x).

4. If all the coefficients in p(x) are integers, then any rational zero of p(x) must have a numerator which is a divisor of k, and a denominator which is a divisor of a.

5. If p(x) is the numerator of a rational function, then the zeros of the rational function are the (complex) numbers which are zeros of p(x) but not of the denominator.

Solving Polynomials and Rational Functions for Zero, Exercise 7. Summary.

Find all zeros of each function, AND factor each function completely. In Problems 9 and 10, factor both the numerator and denominator completely, but do NOT reduce the fraction.

1. $x^3 - 4x^2 - 17x + 60$

2. $x^2 + 10x + 61$

3. $x^4 + 2x^3 - 33x^2 + 22x + 56$

4. $9x^3 + 9x^2 - 16x - 16$

5. $x^5 - 6x^4 + 16x^3 - 32x^2 + 48x - 32$

6. $x^3 - 75x + 88$

7. $2x^4 + 7x^3 - 17x^2 - 10x$

8. $\frac{1}{2}x^3 - 2x^2 + x - \frac{35}{2}$

9. $\frac{x^5 - 6x^4 + 16x^3 - 32x^2 + 48x - 32}{x^2 + 4}$

10. $\frac{x^3 - 1}{x^3 - 8}$

In Problems 11-15, solve the equations.

11. $x^2 + 11x + 30 = x - 31$

12. $9x^3 + 8x^2 - 4 = -x^2 + 16x + 12$

13. $x^3 = 75x - 88$

14. $x^3 - 4x^2 + 2x = 35$

15. $\frac{2x^3 - 9}{x^3 - 8} = 1$

Graphing Polynomial and Rational Functions

A graph is a visual picture of the behavior of a function as the value of the input variable changes. The visual picture is frequently more useful than the explicit calculation used to compute the function value. Polynomial and rational functions are the only functions which can be computed using only addition, subtraction, multiplication, and division. This makes them, in a way, the most basic kinds of functions we have. This chapter will describe methods for building a visual picture (graph) for most polynomial and rational functions.

Part 1 — Transformations

It is possible to accurately graph many functions by starting with the graph of some very basic function and then making simple changes to the graph which result in the graph of the function we are interested in. First, we define the basic functions and their graphs:

1. $f(x) = x$ (this is called the *identity* function).
2. $f(x) = x^n$ when n is even.
3. $f(x) = x^n$ when n is odd (but not equal to 1).
4. $f(x) = \frac{1}{x^n}$ when n is even.
5. $f(x) = \frac{1}{x^n}$ when n is odd (this time including 1).
6. $f(x) = |x|$ (this is not a polynomial or a rational function; but it will provide a good example of some of the rules we want to talk about).

The graphs of these six basic functions are given below.

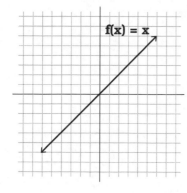

Graph 1.

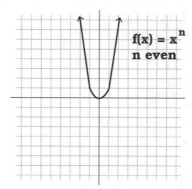

Graph 2

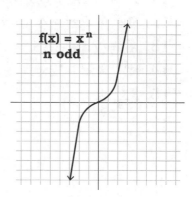

Graph 3

Graph 4	Graph 5	Graph 6
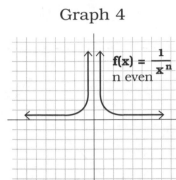	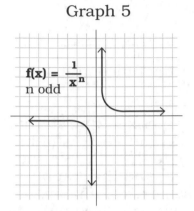	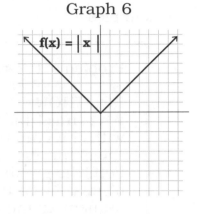

For $f(x) = x^n$, the graph will be very similar to Graph 2 regardless of whether n is equal to 2, 4, or 100, as long as n is even (and positive, of course). The effect of a larger exponent is to make the "U"-shape squarer on the bottom and straighter going up the sides. A similar comment applies to Graphs 3, 4, and 5.

Notice that Graphs 2, 4, and 6 are entirely above (or on) the x-axis. That's because when we raise any number to an even power, or when we take the absolute value of a number, we always get at least zero. Values of y greater than zero are all above the x-axis.

Suppose we want to graph a function f(x), and suppose we can get the formula for f(x) by applying one or more of the changes in the table below to one of our six basic functions. Then the table describes the corresponding changes to the graph.

Change to the function ⟶ Change to the graph

Change to the function	Change to the graph
Add some number c to x.	Shift the graph to the left by c units.
Subtract some number c from x.	Shift the graph to the right by c units.
Replace x by -x.	Reflect the graph in the y-axis (left to right).
Add some number c to f(x).	Shift the graph up by c units.
Subtract some number c from f(x).	Shift the graph down by c units.
Replace f(x) by -f(x).	Reflect the graph in the x-axis (up and down).
Multiply f(x) by a positive number c.	Stretch or shrink the graph vertically by a factor of c.

Problems 1: Graph the function f(x) = $|x + 2|$.

SOLUTION:
We can get the graph of x + 2 by starting with the graph of $|x|$, and then shifting the graph two units to the left. We show both the graph of $|x|$ and the graph of $|x + 2|$ on the same axes. (In subsequent examples, we will show only the new graph – i.e., the graph of the function we want.)

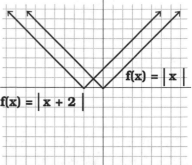

Problem 2: Graph f(x) = $(x - 1)^2$.

SOLUTION:
This will be the graph of f(x) = x^2, shifted to the right by 1 unit.

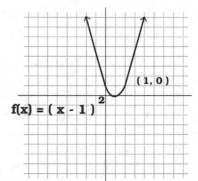

Problem 3: Graph f(x) = $\frac{1}{-x}$.

SOLUTION:
This is the graph of f(x) = $\frac{1}{x}$ reflected in the y-axis. This means that we treat the y-axis like a mirror and reflect everything which is to the right of the y-axis an equal number of units to the left of the axis, and everything which is to the left of the y-axis an equal number of units to the right. Compare the graph to the original f(x) = $\frac{1}{x}$, and the procedure should be clear.

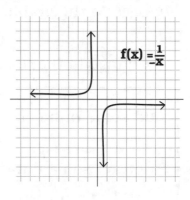

Problem 4: Graph g(x) = $|x|$ + 2.

SOLUTION:
This is the graph of g(x) = $|x|$ shifted up by 2 units. Note that this is *not* the same function, nor the same graph, as we had in Problem 1.

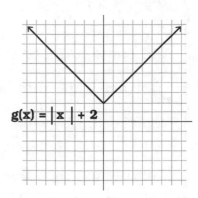

Problem 5: $f(x) = x^2 - 1$.

SOLUTION:
This is the graph of $f(x) = x^2$ shifted down by 1 unit.

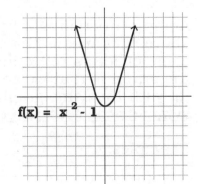

Problem 6: Graph $h(x) = - |x|$.

SOLUTION:
This is the graph of $h(x) = |x|$ reflected in the x-axis. This means we take every part of the graph which is above the x-axis and reflect it an equal distance below the x-axis.

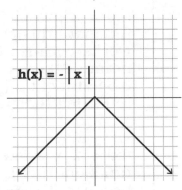

Problem 7: Graph $f(x) = 3|x|$.

SOLUTION:
This is the graph of $y = |x|$ stretched vertically by a factor of 3. *Stretched vertically* means that each point of the original graph ($|x|$) will be moved vertically, 3 times as far away from the x-axis as it was originally. Any point which was originally on the x-axis will stay right where it is.

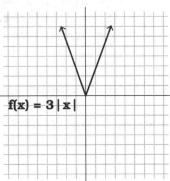

SOLUTION:
This is the graph of $y = x^2$ shrunk vertically by a factor of $\frac{1}{4}$. Shrunk vertically means that each point of the original graph (x^2) will be moved vertically closer to the x-axis, so that the point is only $\frac{1}{4}$ as far from the x-axis as it was originally. Any point which was originally on the x-axis will stay there.

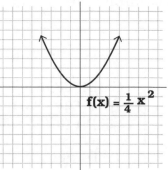

Even and Odd Functions

An <u>even</u> function is a function whose graph does not change when we reflect the graph in the y-axis (left and right). A graph of that kind is said to be <u>symmetrical with respect to the y-axis</u>. According to the preceding transformation rules above, this means the function must not change when we replace x by -x. In fact, another definition of an even function is a function for which $f(-x) = f(x)$.

An <u>odd</u> function is a function such that $f(-x) = -f(x)$. According to the rules above, this means that reflecting the graph in the x-axis would have the same effect as reflecting it in the y-axis. Another geometric description of the graph is that we could spin the graph 180° around the origin, and end up with the same graph we started with. A graph of this kind is said to be <u>symmetrical with respect to the origin</u>.

Examples:

> $f(x) = x^n$, where n is an <u>even</u> number, is an example of an even function (this example is why an even function is called even). This works because $f(-x) = (-x)^n = x^n$ (the minus signs cancel each other because there is an even number of them). A look at the graph of the basic function ($f(x) = x^n$ with n even), given earlier, shows that reflecting the graph in the y-axis would make no change at all.
>
> $f(x) = x^n$, where n is an <u>odd</u> number, is an example of an odd function (this is why they are called odd). This example works because $f(-x) = (-x)^n = -x^n$. Examining the graph of the basic function $f(x) = x^n$ with n odd, we can see that if we spin the graph 180° around the origin, we will come back to the same graph we started with.

Multiple Transformations

It is possible to draw the graphs of more complicated functions by applying several of the transformation rules successively.

Example:

> Draw the graph $f(x) = (3 - x)^4 + 2$.
>
> SOLUTION:
> We begin with the graph of $f(x) = x^4$, and we eventually want the graph of $f(3 - x) + 2$. We work as follows:
>
> 1. To get $f(3 + x)$, we are adding 3 to x, so we move left by 3.
> 2. To get $f(3 - x)$ from $f(3 + x)$, we are replacing x by -x, so we reflect in the y-axis.

3. To get f(3 - x) + 2 from f(3 - x), we are adding 2 to the function, so we move the graph up by 2 units. This last graph will be the one we want.

The three successive graph are as follows:

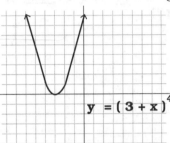 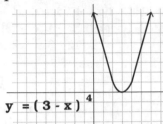 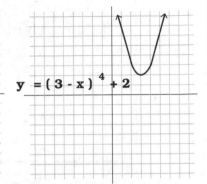

$$y = (3 + x)^4 \qquad y = (3 - x)^4 \qquad y = (3 - x)^4 + 2$$

BIG TIME WARNING

It <u>did</u> matter that we did Step 1 before Step 2. If we had reversed the order, then after Step 1 we would have $f(-x) = (-x)^4$, which is OK. But then in Step 2, if we *add 3 to x* in the function $(-x)^4$, we would get $(-(x + 3))^4$, or $(-x - 3)^4$, which is NOT what we want. Try reflecting in the y-axis first and then moving 3 units left – you will see that you do not have the same graph we had after Step 2. On the other hand, in this problem we could have done Step 3 (moving the graph up 2) at any place in the sequence.

If we are given the graph of a function f(x), we can use the given graph to draw the graph of a modified version of the function, even if we have no formula for the function.

•Example:

Use the graph of f(x) to draw the graph of 3 - f(x - 2).

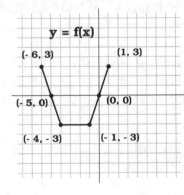

SOLUTION:
We begin from the given graph and perform the following steps:

1. Reflect the x-axis to get -f(x).
2. Move up 3 to get -f(x) + 3 (or 3 - f(x)).
3. Move right by 2 to get 3 - f(x - 2).

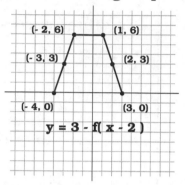

$y = 3 - f(x - 2)$

Graphing Polynomial and Rational Functions, Exercise 1. Transformations.

Graph the following functions:

1. $f(x) = (x + 1)^2$
2. $f(x) = (x - 2)^3$
3. $f(x) = \dfrac{1}{(-x)^2}$
4. $g(x) = \dfrac{1}{x^2} + 3$
5. $g(x) = |x| - \dfrac{1}{2}$
6. $f(x) = -x$
7. $f(x) = 2 - x^4$
8. $f(x) = (2 - x)^4$
9. $f(x) = |-x + 3|$
10. $f(x) = |-x| + 3$

11. Given the following graph of f(x), draw the graphs of:

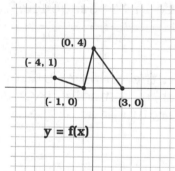

$y = f(x)$

a. f(-x)

b. -f(x)

c. f(x) - 1

d. f(x - 1)

Part 2 | **Graphing Polynomial Functions**

The procedures for graphing polynomials of degree 1 (linear equations) and of degree 2 (quadratic equations) have been covered in the Straightforward Algebra books. Here are several helpful facts for graphing polynomial equations are:

1. The graphs of all polynomial functions are continuous – that is, there are no breaks or gaps in the graph.

2. The entire graph is curved, unless the polynomial has a degree = 1. There will be no straight pieces and no sharp corners.

3. If we travel along a graph from left to right, the graph will be a connected series of uphill and downhill pieces. The total number of uphill and downhill pieces will be <u>at most</u> equal to the degree of the polynomial.

4. The real zeros of the polynomial will be the x-intercepts of the graph. The graph doesn't tell us anything about the (non-real) complex zeros.

5. At the extreme left and the extreme right, the graph will either swoop upward or plunge downward. Which direction the graph goes at the two extremes will depend on two things: the sign of the highest power of x in the polynomial and whether the degree is even or odd. The following chart covers all the possibilities:

Sign of highest power of x	Degree of polynomial	Graph direction at left extreme	Graph direction at right extreme
+	even	up	up
+	odd	down	up
-	even	down	down
-	odd	up	down

If the polynomial factors into linear factors with <u>real</u> zeros, the following procedures can be used:

1. Write the polynomial as a product of linear factors (as described in Chapter 4).

2. For each linear factor, take these steps:
   a. Set the linear factor equal to zero. The answer will be a zero – call it "c" – of the polynomial, and will therefore also be an x-intercept.
   b. Find out what the graph looks like near the x-intercept point (c, o), by substituting $x = c$ into all <u>other</u> linear factors besides the one you are working on at the moment.
   c. Step b will yield either a linear function or a function whose graph can be drawn easily from the rules in Part 1 of this chapter. We draw just a <u>small piece</u> of that graph, a little to the left and right of the x-intercept we are working with.

3. The little pieces drawn in Step 2 will show us what direction the graph goes on either side of the x-intercepts. To determine how far up or down the graph goes between the x-intercepts, substitute an x value halfway between each pair of consecutive x-intercepts. Then you can plot the point halfway between the x-intercepts. This will *not* give us the exact high or low points between the x-intercepts, because calculus is

necessary to precisely locate those points. But the procedure will give a rough approximation.

4. Connect the pieces drawn in Step 2 and the points plotted in Step 3 with a smooth curve. Continue the graph at the extreme left and right in the same direction (upward and downward) it is going at the first and last x-intercept.

•Examples:

Problem 1: Graph the function $x^3 - 2x^2 - 8x$.

SOLUTION:
The function factors as $x(x - 4)(x + 2)$. Therefore the zeros (and x-intercepts) are 0, 4, and -2.

Substituting $x = 0$ into the factors $(x - 4)$ and $(x + 2)$, we find that the function is approximately equal to $x(0 - 4)(0 + 2) = -8x$ in the neighborhood of $(0, 0)$. The exact slope of -8 is not really import-ant, but the fact that it is a <u>negative</u> slope is import-ant – it tells us that the graph is going downhill from left to right as it goes through $(0, 0)$.

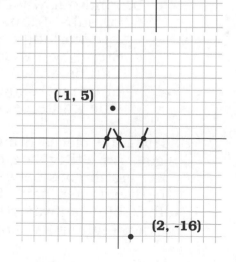

Substituting $x = 4$ into the factors x and $(x + 2)$, we find that the function is approximately equal to $4(x - 4)(4 + 2) = 24x - 96$ in the neighborhood of $(4, 0)$. So we draw a little piece of the graph going through $(4, 0)$ at a slope of positive 24.

Substituting $x = -2$ into the factors x and $(x - 4)$, we find that the function is approximately equal to $-2(-2 - 4)(x + 2) = 12x + 24$ in the neighborhood of $(-2, 0)$. So we draw a little piece of the graph going through $(-2, 0)$ with a steep upward (from left to right) slope.

The halfway point between -2 and 0 is -1. If we substitute -1 into the function, we get $f(-1) = 5$. So we use the point $(-1, 5)$ as the high point on the graph between $(-2, 0)$ and $(0, 0)$. (The actual high point, which can be found by using calculus, is $(-1.10, 5.05)$, to the nearest hundredth). Similarly, we approximate the low point on the graph between $(0, 0)$ and $(4, 0)$ as $(2, -16)$.

The outline of our graph looks like this (note: graph scale reduced to half):

Finally, we draw a smooth curve connecting all the pieces and points that we have plotted, continuing the graph at the left and right in the directions it is going (reduced scale):

(Reduced scale)

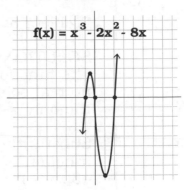

$f(x) = x^3 - 2x^2 - 8x$

Problem 2: Graph the function $x^3 + 2x^2 - 7x + 4$.

SOLUTION:
The function factors as $(x - 1)^2 (x + 4)$. Therefore the zeros and x-intercepts are 1 and -4.

Substituting $x = 1$ into the factor $(x + 4)$, we find that the function is approximately equal to $(x - 1)^2 (1 + 4) = 5(x - 1)^2$, in the neighborhood of $(1, 0)$. From the transformation rules discussed earlier, we know that the graph of $5(x - 1)^2$ is a parabola with its vertex at the point $(1, 0)$. So we draw a little piece of that parabola centered at the point $(1, 0)$.

Substituting $x = -4$ into the factor $(x - 1)$, we find that the function is approximately equal to $(-4 - 1)^2 (x + 4) = 25(x + 4) = 25x + 100$ near the point $(-4, 0)$. So we draw a short piece of straight line through $(-4, 0)$ with a steep upward slope from left to right.

Halfway between -4 and 1 is the number -1.5. If we substitute $x = -1.5$ into the function, we get a function value of 15.625. Therefore, we use the point $(-1.5, 15.625)$ as a <u>rough</u> estimate of the peak of the graph between the two x-intercepts $(-4, 0)$ and $(1, 0)$. Our graph outline now looks like the graph to the right.

• (-1.5, 15.625)

(-4, 0)   (1, 0)

Finally, we connect the pieces of the graph which we have already plotted with a smooth curve:

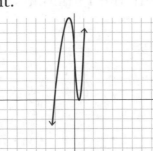

(Reduced Scale)

Problem 3: Graph the function $x^3 - 3x - 52$.

SOLUTION:
The function factors as $(x - 4)(x^2 + 4x + 13)$. The second factor has no real solutions, so the only real zero of the function (and therefore the only x-intercept for the graph) is 4.

Substituting $x = 4$ into the factor $(x^2 + 4x + 13)$, we find that the function is approximately the same as $(x - 4)(16 + 16 + 13) = 45(x - 4) = 45x - 180$, in the neighborhood of $(4, 0)$. Therefore we draw a short straight line through $(4, 0)$, with a steep upward slope from left to right.

To approximate the rest of the graph, we plot points, bearing in mind the rules given at the beginning of Part 2. We know that the graph has at most three uphill and downhill segments, so there is a possibility it will change direction twice. From the facts that the polynomial has odd degree and that the highest power of x is positive, we know that the graph plunges downward at the left end and swoops upward at the right end. We then calculate the following points:

$f(-3) = -70$, so $(-3, -70)$ is on the graph.
$f(-2) = -54$, so $(-2, -54)$ is on the graph.
$f(-1) = -50$, so $(-1, -50)$ is on the graph.
$f(0) \ \ = -52$, so $(0, -52)$ is on the graph.
$f(1) \ \ = -54$, so $(1, -54)$ is on the graph.
$f(2) \ \ = -50$, so $(2, -50)$ is on the graph.
$f(3) \ \ = -34$, so $(3, -34)$ is on the graph.

An examination of these points leads us to guess that the graph turns around somewhere near the point $(-1, -50)$ and again somewhere near $(1, -54)$. As it happens, these guesses are right this time, although again we would need calculus to verify the fact. Given the information we have compiled, our graph now looks like this. Note that the vertical scale has been shrunk to illustrate the important points.

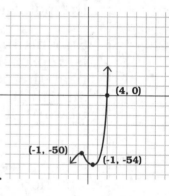

Graphing Polynomial and Rational Functions. Exercise 2. Graphing Polynomial Functions.

Graph the following functions.

1. $x^3 - x^2 + x - 1$

2. $x^3 - 2x^2 - 5x + 6$

3. $x^3 - 2x^2 - 4x$

4. $x^4 - 2x^3 - 4x^2$

5. $x^4 - 6x^2 + 8x - 3$

6. $x^4 - 2x^2 + 1$

7. $-x^4 + 3x^2 + 4$

8. $-x^4 + 4x^3 - 3x^2 - 2x + 6$

9. $x^4 + 8x^3 + 24x^2 + 32x + 16$

10. $x^4 + 3x^3$

Graphing Rational Functions

A rational function is a fraction whose numerator and denominator are polynomials. Technically, a polynomial is a rational function whose denominator is 1, but here in Part 3 we will assume that the denominator has degree 1 or greater – in other words that an x is in the denominator.

The most important difference between graphs of rational functions and graphs of polynomials is the presence of asymptotes in the graphs of rational functions. An **asymptote** to a graph is a straight line which the graph squeezes up against, without actually touching. A good example is the graph $f(x) = \frac{1}{x}$, which was introduced in the first part of this chapter.

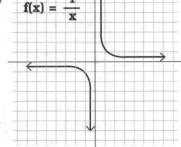

Notice that the graph of $y = \frac{1}{x}$ squeezes up against the x-axis and the y-axis, although the graph never intersects either axis. Both the x-axis and the y-axis are asymptotes to the graph of $f(x) = \frac{1}{x}$.

There are two categories of asymptotes for graphs of rational functions: **vertical asymptotes**, and **horizontal** or **slant asymptotes**.

How to Find Vertical Asymptotes

Recall that the equation of any vertical straight line in the plane is x = c, where c is some number. The vertical asymptotes of the graph of a rational function are the lines x = c, where c's are the *real* zeros of the denominator of the function. Once again, the graph of $y = \frac{1}{x}$ is a simple example. Zero is the only zero of the denominator, and the only vertical asymptote is x = 0 (otherwise known as the y-axis).

•Example:

Find the vertical asymptotes of the graph $g(x) = \frac{x-5}{x^4-3x^2-4}$.

SOLUTION:
By using the procedure learned in Chapter 4, we find that the only real zeros of $x^4 - 3x^2 - 4$ are 2 and -2 (remember that non-real zeros don't show up on graphs – this rule also applies to finding asymptotes). Therefore the lines x = -2 and x = 2 are vertical asymptotes of the graph of this function.

The Appearance of a Graph Near a Vertical Asymptotes

The graph of a rational function will squeeze against a vertical asymptote on both sides. On either side, the graph will either swoop upward or plunge downward against the asymptote. The appearance of a graph near a vertical asymptotes has four possibilities:

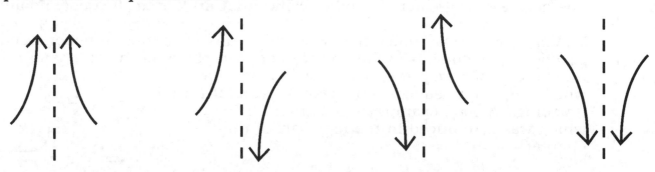

Here is a procedure for deciding which of the four illustrations above to use in drawing a graph near the vertical asymptote x = c: Evaluate the function at a number slightly less than c, and again at a number slightly greater than c. If the calculated function value is positive, the graph swoops upward toward the asymptote. If the calculated value is negative, the graph plunges downward toward the asymptote.

•Example:

The graphs of $\frac{x^2}{x-2}$, $\frac{x+1}{(x-2)^2}$, $\frac{1-x}{x-2}$, and $\frac{2-x^3}{(x-2)^2}$ each have a vertical asymptote at x = 2. Draw the graphs near the vertical asymptote.

SOLUTION:

If $f(x) = \frac{x^2}{x-2}$, then f(1.99) = -396.01, and f(2.01) = 404.01. Therefore the graph plunges down to the left of x = 2, and swoops up from the right.

If $f(x) = \frac{x+1}{(x-2)^2}$ then f(1.99) = 29900, and f(2.01) = 30100. Therefore the graph swoops up toward the asymptote x = 2 on both sides.

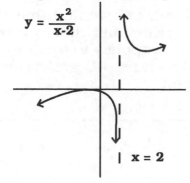

$y = \frac{x^2}{x-2}$

x = 2

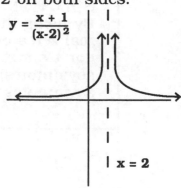

$y = \frac{x+1}{(x-2)^2}$

x = 2

If $f(x) = \frac{1-x}{x-2}$, then $f(1.99) = 99$, and $f(2.01) = -101$. Therefore the graph swoops up toward the asymptote from the left, and plunges down from the right.

If $f(x) = \frac{2-x^3}{(x-2)^2}$, then $f(1.99) = -58805.99$, and $f(2.01) = -61206.01$. Therefore the graph plunges downward toward the asymptote from both sides.

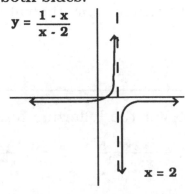

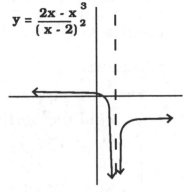

Horizontal or Slant Asymptotes

If the graph of a rational functon has a horizontal or slant asymptote, then the graph will squeeze up against that asymptote at the right and left extremes of the graph – that is, as x gets very large in a positive or negative direction. So one way of finding a horizontal or slant asymptote is to examine what happens to the function as x gets either huge positive or huge negative. HOWEVER: unfortunately, we cannot just evaluate the function at a large negative and a large positive number. If, for example, the line y = 3x - 8 is a slant asymptote, then we will probably get approximately 2989 if the function is evaluated at x = 999. But that will not tell us that the asymptote is y = 3x - 8!

A procedure for finding a horizontal or slant asymptote is this: Divide the numerator of the function, c(x), by the denominator, d(x), using the procedure for polynomial division as presented in Chapter 4. If we let q(x) = the quotient and r(x) = the remainder which we get when we do the division, then we have the equation:

$$\frac{n(x)}{d(x)} = q(x) + \frac{r(x)}{d(x)}$$

NOTE: if the degree of n(x), the numerator, is less than the degree of the denominator d(x), then the quotient will be zero, and the remainder r(x) will be the numerator itself. In any case, the degree of the remainder r(x) will always be less than the degree of the denominator d(x), and therefore the expression $\frac{r(x)}{d(x)}$ will approach zero as x gets huge in either the positive or negative direction (more about this below). Therefore the rational function itself, $\frac{n(x)}{d(x)}$, will approach the quotient q(x) as x gets huge positive or huge negative. If the equation y = q(x) is a linear equation, then the graph of y = q(x) is the horizontal or slant asymptote for the graph. If q(x) has degree 2 or greater, then there is no horizontal or slant asymptote.

(Optional) Explanation of Why $\frac{r(x)}{d(x)}$ Approaches Zero as x Gets Huge

Suppose x is huge. Then any power of x is enormously bigger than any lower power of x. For example, if x = 9 million, then x^3 will be 9 million times bigger than x^2. Thus, if the denominator has a larger degree than the numerator, the denominator will be enormously bigger than the numerator when x gets big enough. Even if the numerator has large coefficients, we can choose x values big enough to dwarf the size of the coefficients. When a denominator is enormously bigger than the numerator, the value of the fraction is close to zero.

•Examples:

Find the horizontal or slant asymptote for the following functions:

a. $\dfrac{3x^2+2x-5}{x^2-4}$ b. $\dfrac{3x^2+2x-5}{4-x^3}$ c. $\dfrac{3x^3+2x^2-5}{x^2-4}$ d. $\dfrac{3x^4+2x^2-5}{x^2-4}$

SOLUTIONS:

a. If we divide the denominator into the numerator as explained in Chapter 4, our quotient q(x) is 3. Therefore the line y = 3 is a horizontal asymptote for the graph.

b. When we divide the denominator into the numerator in this one, the quotient is zero because the degree of the divisor is greater than the degree of the dividend. Therefore the line y = 0 is a horizontal asymptote for this function. (The line y = 0 is just another name for the x-axis.)

c. When we divide the numerator by the denominator in this case, the quotient is 3x + 2. Therefore the line y = 3x + 2 is a slant asymptote for the graph of this function (we call this one a slant asymptote rather than a horizontal asymptote because y = 3x + 2 is not horizontal. The lines y = 0 and y = 3, from the previous two examples, are horizontal.)

d. After dividing the numerator by the denominator this time, the quotient is $3x^2 + 14$. Since $y = 3x^2 + 14$ is not a linear equation, there is no horizontal or slant asymptote for the graph of this function.

The Appearance of a Graph as it Approaches a Horizontal or Slant Asymptote

If the graph of a rational function has a horizontal or slant asymptote, the graph will approach that asymptote at both the extreme left and the extreme right of the graph. At either end, the graph can approach the asymptote from above or from below. This means we choose one of the four following possibilities:

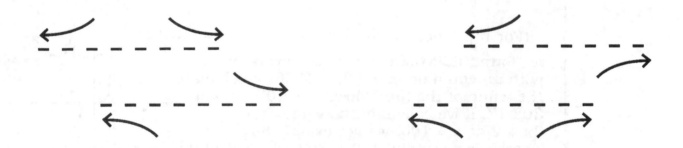

We can tell whether the graph approaches a horizontal or slant asymptote from above or below by plotting one point of the graph for a large positive value of x, and another point for a large negative value. We can assume that if the point we plot is above the asymptote, the graph will approach the asymptote from above, and if the point is below the asymptote, the graph will approach the asymptote from below.

•Example:

Sketch the graphs for the functions a, b, and c from the examples on page 84, as they approach the horizontal or slant asymptote.

SOLUTION:

a. For the function $\frac{3x^2+2x-5}{x^2-4}$, we found that the asymptote is y = 3. If we calculate the value of the function for x = 100, we get 3.0207. Since the point (100, 3.0207) is above the line y = 3, we assume that the graph approaches the asymptote from above as it goes to the right. On the other hand, if we calculate the value of the function for x = -100, we get 2.9807, which is less than 3. The graph approaches the asymptote from below as it goes to the left.

$$y = \frac{3x^2 + 2x - 5}{x^2 - 4}$$

y = 3

x = -2   x = 2

b. For the function $\frac{3x^2+2x-5}{4-x^3}$, we found that the horizontal asymptote is the x-axis, or the line y = 0. If we substitute x = 100 into the function, we get -.0302 (less than zero). If we substitute x = -100, we get .0298 (greater than zero). The graph approaches the horizontal asymptote from above on the left, and from below on the right.

$$y = \frac{3x^2 + 2x - 5}{4 - x^3}$$

$x = \sqrt[3]{4}$

85

c. For the function $\frac{3x^3+2x^2-5}{x^2-4}$, $\quad y = \frac{3x^3+2x^2-5}{x^2-4}$

we found that there is a slant asymptote, with an equation of $y = 3x + 2$. If we calculate the value of the function at $x = 100$, we get 302.12; if we calculate the value of $3x + 2$ at $x = 100$, we get exactly 302. Therefore the point (100, 302.12) is slightly above the line $y = 3x + 2$, and the graph approaches the slant asymptote from above on the right. If we substitute $x = -100$ into the function, we get -298.12. Substituting $x = -100$ into $3x + 2$ gives -298. The point (-100, -298.12) is therefore slightly below the line $y = 3x + 2$, and so the graph must approach the slant asymptote from below at the left.

BIG TIME WARNING

A horizontal or slant asymptote has <u>no</u> effect on the graph except at the right and left extremes. In particular, it is NOT TRUE that a graph can never cross its horizontal or slant asymptote. The graph might cross the horizontal or slant asymptote many times toward "middle" of the graph. Only when the graph make its "final approach" to the asymptote, at the left and right extremes of the graph, will it squeeze up against the asymptote without ever touching it. (By the way, it <u>is</u> true that the graph can never touch one of its <u>vertical</u> asymptotes.)

Helpful Facts for Drawing Graphs of Rational Functions

1. The graph is broken into pieces by the vertical asymptotes. Between the vertical asymptotes, the graph is continuous and can be handled much like the graph of a polynomial.

2. The x-intercepts (if any) of the graph of a rational function occur at the point(s) where the function = 0. A RATIONAL FUNCTION EQUALS ZERO WHEN AND ONLY WHEN THE NUMERATOR EQUALS ZERO. THE GRAPHS OF $\frac{2}{x-5}$ AND $\frac{x^2+5}{2x^2-18}$ HAVE NO X-INTERCEPTS.

3. If the denominator has no x, then the function is really a polynomial. For example $\frac{3x+4}{7}$ is really $\frac{3}{7}x + \frac{4}{7}$.

4. If there is no horizontal or slant asymptote, we draw the graph at the left and right extremes the same way we do for a polynomial: we check a large positive and a large negative value of x to see whether the graph swoops upward or plunges downward at the left and right extremes.

Procedure for Graphing Rational Functions (Putting It All Together)

1. Find the zeros of the denominator, and use the answer(s) to draw the vertical asymptote(s) with dotted lines.

2. Use the procedure given earlier to find and draw the horizontal or slant asymptote, if any.

3. Find the zeros of the numerator, and use them to plot the x-intercepts. Then use the procedure discussed in Part 2 (Graphing Polynomial Functions) to draw a short piece of the graph near the x-intercept.

4. Use the procedure given earlier to decide what the graph looks like near the vertical asymptote(s), and appropriately draw short pieces of the graph as the graph approaches each vertical asymptote from the left and right.

5. Use the procedure given earlier to decide what the graph looks like near the horizontal or slant asymptote, if there is one. Then draw short pieces of the graph at the left and right extremes as the graph approaches the asymptote.

6. If the graph has no horizontal or slant asymptote, determine what happens to the graph at the left and right extremes by substituting a large positive and a large negative number for x, just as we did in the section about polynomials. Then draw short pieces of the graph at the left and right extremes.

7. Connect the pieces of the graph which you have already drawn (including the x-intercepts), with a smooth curve. Remember that the graph cannot go through the x-axis except at the x-intercepts which you have already plotted. Also remember that the only breaks in the graph are at the vertical asymptotes. To accomplish this step, it is sometimes desirable to substitute a value for x halfway between a vertical asymptote and an x-intercept, or between two vertical asymptotes, to see what is happening to the function on that interval.

•Example:

Sketch the graph of the function $f(x) = \frac{x+3}{x^2+4x-5}$.

SOLUTION:

We will take the exact same steps as in the procedure above, listing them in the same order:

1. By using the procedures from Chapter 4, we find that the

denominator factors into (x + 5) (x - 1), and that the zeros are -5 and 1. The vertical asymptotes for our graph are x = -5 and x = 1. We draw these two dotted lines on the graph.

2. If we divide the denominator into the numerator, we get a quotient of zero, because the degree of the denominator is greater than the degree of the numerator. Therefore the line y = 0 is the horizontal asymptote for the graph. Since the line y = 0 is the x-axis, drawing a dotted line over it would not accomplish anything. We will just have to remember that the x-axis is the horizontal asymptote.

3. The only zero of the numerator is -3. Plot the point (-3, 0) on the graph as the only x-intercept.

4. f(-5.01) is about -33.4, so the graph plunges downward toward the vertical asymptote x = -5 as it approaches the asympotote from the left. f(-4.99) is approximately 33.2, so the graph swoops upward toward the line x = -5 as it approaches the asymptote from the right. Similar calculations give f(.99) = about -66.6, and f(1.01) = about 66.7, which means that as the graph approaches the asymptote x = 1, it goes downward from the left and upward from the right. We draw four short pieces of the graph to represent the approaches to the vertical asymptotes.

5. f(-100) is about -0.01, and f(100) is about 0.01, so the graph approaches the horizontal asymptote (y = 0) from below on the left, and from above on the right. We draw short pieces of the graph at the left and right extremes to illustrate the approaches to the asymptote.

6. Step 6 applies only in the case where there is no horizontal or slant asymptote.

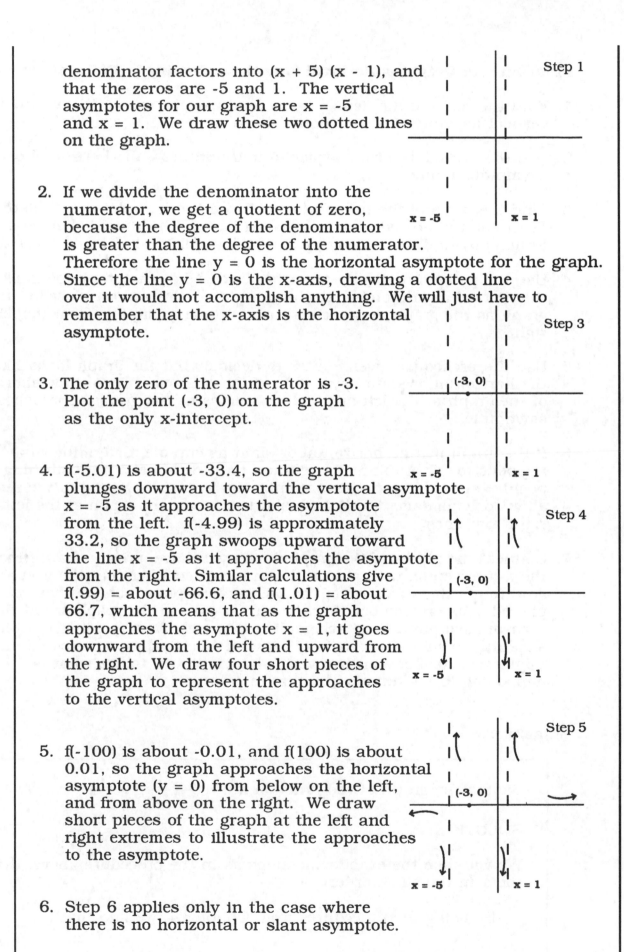

7. In this instance, there is no real need to plot any
   additional points. We can get a fairly accurate
   picture of the graph by simply connecting
   the parts of the graph which we have aready
   drawn.

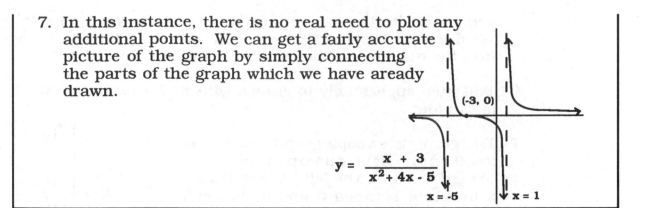

$$y = \frac{x + 3}{x^2 + 4x - 5}$$

(-3, 0)

x = -5   x = 1

•Example:

Sketch the graph of f(x) = $\dfrac{x^3 - x^2 - 16x - 20}{x^2 - 4x}$.

SOLUTION:

1. The denominator factors as x(x - 4). The zeros of the
   denominator are 0 and 4. The two vertical asymptotes
   are x = 0 (the y-axis) and x = 4. We draw a dotted line for x = 4,
   and keep in mind that the y-axis is also a vertical asymptote.

2. If we divide the numerator by the denominator, the quotient is
   x + 3 (with a remainder of -4x - 20, but we don't care about that).
   Therefore the line y = x + 3 is the slant asymptote for our graph.
   Draw that asymptote as a dotted line.

3. By using the procedures from Chapter 4, we find that -2 and 5 are
   the two real zeros of the numerator. We plot the points (-2, 0) and
   (5, 0) as the only two x-intercepts for the graph.

4. To determine what the graph looks like near the vertical
   asymptotes (x = 0 and x = 4), we calculate approximately that
   f(-0.01) = -495, f(0.01) = 505, f(3.99) = 908, and f(4.01) = -892.
   Our conclusions are that for the asymptote x = 0, the graph
   approaches it downwards from the left and upward from the right;
   for the asymptote x = 4, the graph approaches it upward from the
   left and downward from the right. We draw the appropriate short
   pieces of the graph near those two asymptotes.

5. To determine what the graph looks like as it approaches the slant
   asymptote y = x + 3 at the left and right extremes, we calculate
   that f(-199) is about -195.98, and f(199) is about 201.98. So our
   graph will contain the point (-199, -195.98), which is above the
   point (-199, -196) on the line y = x + 3. Therefore the graph
   approaches the slant asymptote from above as it goes to the left.
   Also, our graph contains the point (199, 201.98), which is below
   the point (199, 202) on the line y = x + 3. So our graph

will approach the slant asymptote from below as it goes to the right. We draw the two short pieces of the graph as the graph goes off into the distance at the left and right extremes.

6. This step applies only to graphs with no horizontal or slant asymptote.

7. The graph is swooping up toward x = 0 on the right, and up again toward x = 4 on the left. There is no x-intercept between 0 and 4. Therefore as the graph travels from x = 0 toward x = 4, it must go downward and then turn around at some point without crossing the x-axis to head back up toward the line x = 4. Calculus is required to identify the turnaround precisely, but we can approximate the point halfway between the two asymptotes, at x = 2. We can calculate that f(2) = 12, so we plot the turnaround point at (2, 12) (the actual correct point is about (1.45, 11.43)). Smoothly connect all pieces and points that we have plotted, ending up with our sketch.

Graphing Polynomial and Rational Functions, Exercise 3. Graphing Rational Functions.

Sketch the graph of each function.

1. $\dfrac{x-2}{x+1}$

2. $\dfrac{x-2}{x^2-1}$

3. $\dfrac{x-2}{x^2-1}$

4. $\dfrac{x^2-1}{x-2}$

5. $\dfrac{x}{x^2-5}$

6. $\dfrac{x-6}{x^2-5}$

7. $\dfrac{x^3}{x^2-20}$

8. $\dfrac{x^2-20}{x^3}$

9. $\dfrac{x^3+7x^2+7x+6}{2x^2-5x-12}$

10. $\dfrac{2x^2-5x-12}{x^3+7x^2+7x+6}$

11. $\dfrac{5x^2+8x-4}{2x^2+x-28}$

12. $\dfrac{2x^2+x-28}{5x^2+8x-4}$

Trigonometric Functions

It is assumed that the reader is familiar with the material presented in *Straightforward Trigonometry*. That book defined trigonometric functions of acute angles based on the ratio of sides of right triangles. Here we will define trigonometric functions of arbitrary angles of any size, and then expand the definition so that we can use any number as an input to a trigonometic function, without reference to any angle at all.

Trigonometric functions have many interesting properties which polynomial and rational functions do not have, and they are frequently used to describe naturally occurring functions in science and engineering.

Part 1 — Trigonometric Functions of Any Angle

Angles in Standard Position

An angle is said to be in **standard position** if the two sides of the angle are placed in an x-y coordinate plane, with the vertex of the angle at the origin, and one side (referred to as in the *initial side*) coinciding with the positive x-axis. The other side of the angle (called the *terminal side*) is positioned in the following manner: If the angle is zero degrees, then the terminal side also coincides with the positive x-axis. For angles with a positive number of degrees, we rotate the terminal side <u>counter-clockwise</u> from its beginning position along the positive x-axis, through the number of degrees called for by the angle. If the angle is greater than 360 degrees, we just continue to rotate past the original position until we have rotated through the angle we need. This means, for example, that the terminal side of a 456-degree angle will be in the same position as the terminal side of a 96-degree angle. If the angle is a negative number of degrees, we do the same thing except we rotate the terminal side <u>*clockwise*</u> from its original position along the positive x-axis.

•Example

Show the angles 45°, 210°, and -405° in standard position.

SOLUTION:

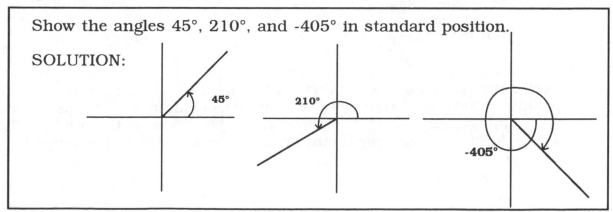

91

In addition to the three standard trigonometric functions (sine, cosine, and tangent), there are three more trigonometric functions that can be defined as reciprocals of the original three functions:

$$\text{secant } x = \frac{1}{\text{cosine } x} = \frac{\text{hypotenuse}}{\text{adjacent}}$$

$$\text{cosecant } x = \frac{1}{\text{sine } x} = \frac{\text{hypotenuse}}{\text{opposite}}$$

$$\text{cotangent } x = \frac{1}{\text{tangent } x} = \frac{\text{adjacent}}{\text{opposite}}$$

The secant, cosecant, and cotangent functions are abbreviated **sec**, **csc**, and **cot** respectively.

Trigonometric Functions of Acute Angles in Standard Position

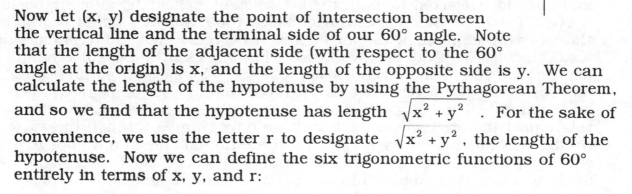

Consider an angle of 60°, placed in a standard position in the x-y plane. Now draw a vertical line upwards from any point on the positive x-axis until the vertical line intersects the terminal side of our 60° angle. Notice that we now have a right triangle, whose three sides are the positive x-axis, the terminal side of our 60° angle, and the vertical line we just drew.

Now let (x, y) designate the point of intersection between the vertical line and the terminal side of our 60° angle. Note that the length of the adjacent side (with respect to the 60° angle at the origin) is x, and the length of the opposite side is y. We can calculate the length of the hypotenuse by using the Pythagorean Theorem, and so we find that the hypotenuse has length $\sqrt{x^2 + y^2}$. For the sake of convenience, we use the letter r to designate $\sqrt{x^2 + y^2}$, the length of the hypotenuse. Now we can define the six trigonometric functions of 60° entirely in terms of x, y, and r:

$$\sin 60° = \frac{\text{opp}}{\text{hyp}} = \frac{y}{r} \qquad\qquad \sec 60° = \frac{\text{hyp}}{\text{adj}} = \frac{r}{x}$$

$$\cos 60° = \frac{\text{adj}}{\text{hyp}} = \frac{x}{r} \qquad\qquad \csc 60° = \frac{\text{hyp}}{\text{opp}} = \frac{r}{y}$$

$$\tan 60° = \frac{\text{opp}}{\text{adj}} = \frac{y}{x} \qquad\qquad \cot 60° = \frac{\text{adj}}{\text{opp}} = \frac{x}{y}$$

Notice that no matter what vertical line we choose to draw upward from the positive x-axis, we would get the same trigonometric functions, because we would always have a right triangle with a 60° angle at the origin. Therefore, we could have chosen <u>any</u> point on the terminal side of the angle to be (x, y).

Trigonometric Functions of Arbitrary Angles

The procedure for defining the six trigonometric functions of any angle is:

1. Place the angle in standard position in the x-y plane as shown earlier.

2. Choose any convenient point (other than the origin) on the terminal side to be the point (x, y).

3. Let $r = \sqrt{x^2 + y^2}$. Note that r, unlike x and y, is <u>always positive</u>.

4. Now the definitions of the six trigonometric functions are:

$$\sin = \frac{y}{r} \qquad\qquad \sec = \frac{r}{x}$$

$$\cos = \frac{x}{r} \qquad\qquad \csc = \frac{r}{y}$$

$$\tan = \frac{y}{x} \qquad\qquad \cot = \frac{x}{y}$$

•Example:

Find the six trigonometric functions of an angle whose terminal side contains the point (-5, 12).

SOLUTION:

We are given x = -5 and y = 12. We calculate $r = \sqrt{(-5)^2 + 12^2} = 13$. Let us designate the angle itself by the letter A. Then we calculate:

$$\sin A = \frac{12}{13} \qquad\qquad \sec A = \frac{13}{-5} = \frac{-13}{5}$$

$$\cos A = \frac{-5}{13} \qquad\qquad \csc A = \frac{13}{12}$$

$$\tan A = \frac{12}{-5} = \frac{-12}{5} \qquad\qquad \cot A = \frac{-5}{12}$$

Important Fact

It should be clear from the discussion above that any two angles which have the same terminal side have the same trigonometric function values. For example, sin 387° = sin 27°, because when we draw an angle of 387° in standard position, we rotate around the origin one full rotation and then an additional 27°.

Quadrants

The x-axis and y-axis divide the entire plane up into four rectangular sectors, called **quadrants**. The "northeast" (upper right) sector is called the first quadrant or QI. The second, third, and fourth quadrants are the upper left, lower left, and lower right quadrants respectively.

QII	QI
QIII	QIV

If we know that a point is in a certain quadrant, we know the signs of both the x- and y-coordinates.

Quadrant	x	y
I	+	+
II	–	+
III	–	–
IV	+	–

Since r is always positive, we can determine the sign of each of the six trigonometric functions if we know the quadrant which the terminal side lives in. For instance, the tangent of a QIII angle is always positive because y and x will both be negative. The sine of a QIV angle is negative because y will be negative and r positive.

	QI	QII	QIII	QIV
sine	+	+	–	–
cosine	+	–	–	+
tangent	+	–	+	–
secant	+	–	–	+
cosecant	+	+	–	–
cotangent	+	–	+	–

Trigonometric Functions of Special Angles

The trigonometric functions of 30°, 60°, and 45° can be found by applying some facts from elementary geometry to right triangles containing those angles. Diagrams of those triangles are shown here:

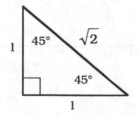 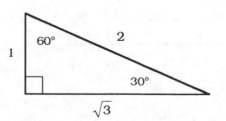

From the diagram, we can fill in this table:

	sin	cos	tan	sec	csc	cot
30°	$\frac{1}{2}$	$\frac{\sqrt{3}}{2}$	$\frac{1}{\sqrt{3}}$	$\frac{2}{\sqrt{3}}$	2	$\sqrt{3}$
60°	$\frac{\sqrt{3}}{2}$	$\frac{1}{2}$	$\sqrt{3}$	2	$\frac{2}{\sqrt{3}}$	$\frac{1}{\sqrt{3}}$
45°	$\frac{1}{\sqrt{2}}$	$\frac{1}{\sqrt{2}}$	1	$\sqrt{2}$	$\sqrt{2}$	1

Reference Angles

As long as an angle's terminal side lies inside one of the four quadrants instead of along one of the axes, there is an acute angle between the terminal side and the x-axis. This acute angle is called the **reference angle** for the original angle. Reference angles have some important properties:

    1. A reference angle is always between 0° and 90°.

    2. A reference angle is always positive. It doesn't matter from which direction we draw it, and it doesn't matter whether we draw it from the positive or the negative x-axis.

    3. Most important, the six trigonometric functions of a reference angle have exactly the same value as the trigonometric functions of the original angle, <u>except possibly for the plus and minus</u>.

The following diagram illustrates the situation in the case of angle A from the example on page 93. The reference angle R is an angle of the right triangle QRP. The hypotenuse of the triangle is 13, the side opposite R is 12, and the side adjacent to R has the length of 5 (not -5; this is just an old-fashioned triangle that never heard of negative lengths).

Therefore the trigonometric functions of R are exactly the same as they are for A, except that all the trigonometric functions of R have positive values.

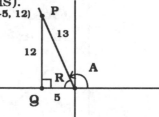

•Example:

    Calculate the six trigonometric functions of -145° (figures in diagram are approximate).

SOLUTION:

35° is the reference angle for -145°.
From the diagram, the six trigonometric functions of 35° are:

$$\sin 35° = \frac{7}{12.2} = .574 \qquad \sec 35° = \frac{12.2}{10} = 1.220$$

$$\cos 35° = \frac{10}{12.2} = .820 \qquad \csc 35° = \frac{12.2}{7} = 1.74$$

$$\tan 35° = \frac{7}{10} = .700 \qquad \cot 35° = \frac{10}{7} = 1.43$$

Now, -145° is a QIII angle. The tangent and cotangent of -145° are positive, and the other four functions are negative. Thus the six trigonometric functions of -145° are:

$$\sin(-145°) = -.574 \qquad \sec(-145°) = -1.220$$
$$\cos(-145°) = -.820 \qquad \csc(-145°) = -1.74$$
$$\tan(-145°) = .700 \qquad \cot(-145°) = 1.43$$

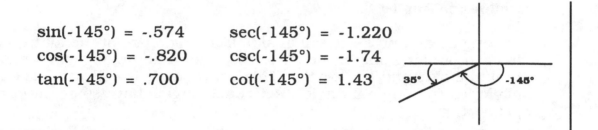

•Example:

Use a reference angle to calculate sin 135°, cos(-120°), and tan 330°.

SOLUTION:

The reference angle for 135° is 45°. The sine is positive in QII. Therefore, $\sin 135° = \sin 45° = \frac{1}{\sqrt{2}}$.

The reference angle for -120° is 60°. The cosine is negative in QIII, so $\cos(-120°) = -\cos 60° = -\frac{1}{2}$.

Finally, the reference angle for 330° is 30°, and the tangent is negative in the fourth quadrant, so $\tan 330° = -\tan 30° = -\frac{1}{\sqrt{3}}$.

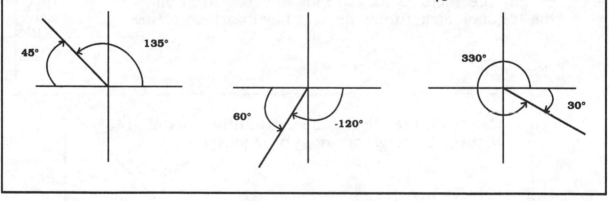

Quadrantal Angles

If an angle in which we are interested is a multiple of 90°, then the terminal side will coincide with either the x-axis or the y-axis. Such angles are called **quadrantal angles** (a strange name, since these are the only angles which do not lie in any quadrant!). For any quadrantal angle, the easiest point to choose on the terminal side is one of the four: (-1, 0), (1, 0), (0, -1), or (0, 1).

•Examples:

> Find all six trigonometric functions of the angles 720° and -90°.
>
> SOLUTION:
>
> The terminal of a 720° angle in standard position is the positive x-axis. Therefore we choose the point (1, 0) as (x, y), and $r = \sqrt{x^2 + 0^2} = 1$. Using x = 1, y = 0, and r = 1, the six trigonometric functions for 720° are:
>
> 30°
>
> $$\begin{array}{ll} \sin 720° = 0 & \sec 720° = 1 \\ \cos 720° = 1 & \csc 720° = \text{undefined} \\ \tan 720° = 0 & \cot 720° = \text{undefined} \end{array}$$
>
> The terminal side of a -90° angle in standard position is the negative y-axis. Therefore we can choose the point (0, -1) to define the trigonometric functions. We get $r = \sqrt{0^2 + (-1)^2} = 1$. Using x = 0, y = -1, r = 1, we get:
>
> $$\begin{array}{ll} \sin(-90°) = -1 & \sec(-90°) = \text{undefined} \\ \cos(-90°) = 0 & \csc(-90°) = -1 \\ \tan(-90°) = \text{undefined} & \cot(-90°) = 0 \end{array}$$

Important Note on Algebraic Expressions Involving Trigonometric Functions

If we want to raise a trigonometric function value to a power, we usually write the exponent right after the function abbreviation. For example, $\cos^3 58°$ means $(\cos 58°)^3$. THIS RULE DOES NOT APPLY WHEN THE EXPONENT IS -1. An exponent of -1 is reserved for a special purpose to be described in Part 3 of this chapter. If we want to express the -1 power of $\tan 123°$, for example, we have to do it by writing $(\tan 123°)^{-1}$ (or else $\cot 123°$, which is the same thing).

Trigonometric Functions, Exercise 1. Trigonometric Functions of Any Angle.

1. Find the six trigonometric functions of an angle whose terminal side in standard position contains the point (4, -3).

2. Find the six trigonometric functions (to the nearest thousandth) of an angle whose terminal side in standard position contains the point (-5, -7).

3. Find the six trigonometric functions (to the nearest thousandth) of an angle whose terminal side contains the point (8, 11).

4. Find the six trigonometric functions (to the nearest thousandth) of an angle whose terminal side contains the point (-5, 0).

5. Suppose cot A = 4.705, and csc A = -4.810. What quadrant is the terminal side of A in?

97

6. Suppose the terminal side of angle B is not in the first quadrant, and suppose cos B = 0.345. Where is the terminal side of angle B?

7. What is the reference angle for -600°?

8. What is the reference angle for 25°?

9. What is the reference angle for 550°?

10. Given the following:

sin 75° = 0.966	sin(-75°) = -0.966	sin 15° = 0.259
cos 75° = 0.259	cos(-75°) = 0.259	cos 15° = 0.966
tan 75° = 3.732	tan(-75°) = -3.732	tan 15° = 0.268

Find all six trigonometric functions of 255°.

11. Use the diagram below to calculate the values of the six trigonometric functions of -393.7°.

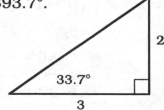

12. Find the six trigonometric functions of -270°.

<table>
<tr><td>Part 2</td><td>Trigonometric Functions of Real Numbers</td></tr>
</table>

Radians

Angles are not always measured in degrees. There is another commonly used unit of measure called the **radian**. A degree is defined by dividing one full circular rotation into 360°. A radian is defined by dividing a full rotation into 2π (about 6.28) radians. One radian is equal to about 57.3°. The radian seems like an awkward unit to use for measuring angles, but for many purposes (especially calculus), the radian is a much simpler and easier measure. Geometrically, the radian is a useful measure when dealing with problems involving circles. Two examples arise from the diagram to the right, where we have a circle of radius r, and a central angle C. Central angle C intercepts an arc of the circle (length L) and bounds a sector of the circle whose area is A. If (and only if) we measure angle C in radians, we can calculate the length of arc L and the sector area A with the following formulas:

$$A = \tfrac{1}{2}r^2 C \qquad\qquad L = r C$$

If we let D = the measure of an angle in degrees, and R = measure of the same angle in radians, then the formulas for converting radians to degrees (and vice versa) are:

$$R = \frac{\pi}{180}D \qquad\qquad D = \frac{\pi}{180}R$$

•Examples:

Convert a 123° angle to radians, and a -4 radian angle to degrees.

SOLUTION:

$$R = \frac{\pi}{180}(123) = \frac{123}{180}\pi \ (\approx 2.147) \text{ radians}$$
$$D = \frac{180}{\pi}(-4) = \frac{-720}{\pi} \ (\approx -229.18) \text{ degrees}$$

NOTE: Normally, if π is a factor or denominator in the measure of an angle, we leave the π symbol as part of the value, rather than express it with a decimal approximation. So we give the answers as written above instead of 2.147 radians and -229.183 degrees.

Special Angles Expressed in Radians

Angles of 0°, 30°, 45°, 60°, 90°, and 180° are used so frequently that it is useful to become familiar with the radian measure of those same angles:

degrees	radians
0°	0
30°	$\frac{\pi}{6}$
45°	$\frac{\pi}{4}$
60°	$\frac{\pi}{3}$
90°	$\frac{\pi}{2}$
180°	π

Trigonometric Functions of Real Numbers

Until now, the six trigonometric functions have been defined by using an angle as input. Now we will define the trigonometric functions of any real number x:

Let x be any real number. Then the sine of x (abbreviated sin x) is equal to the sine of an angle of size x radians.

The other five trigonometric functions of real numbers are defined similarly. Thus, the expression "tan x" has no ambiguity. If we see the expression "tan 27", we do not ask, "27 degrees or 27 radians?". The answer is "<u>neither</u>". It is simply the tangent of the <u>number</u> 27 (which happens to be about -3.274). It is true that the tangent of the number 27 is the same as the tangent of a 27-radian angle, but tan 27 means tangent of the <u>number</u> 27 – unless we are doing a geometric problem involving a specified angle.

BIG TIME WARNING

Don't ever, <u>ever</u>, EVER, say (or even think!) tangent <u>times</u> 27!! The word "tangent" does NOT refer to a number which can be multiplied – it refers to a <u>function</u>. The same warning, of course, applies to the other five trigonometric functions. In particular, sin(x + y) does not distribute as sinx + siny!

A Note on Using a Calculator to Find Trigonometric Functions

Most calculator screens display a tiny "DEG" when the calculator assumes that trigonometric functions are being calculated for angles in degrees, and RAD when the functions are calculated for angles in radians or real numbers. Most calculators have a key labeled "DRG". To get trigonometric functions of real numbers or of angles measured in radians, press the DRG key until the screen displays "RAD".

Trigonometric Functions, Exercise 2. Trigonometric Functions of Real Numbers.

1. Express 40° in radians.
2. Express -495° in radians.
3. Express $\frac{3\pi}{4}$ radians in degrees.
4. Express $-\frac{3}{5}$ radians in degrees.
5. Find $\sin\frac{2\pi}{3}$.
6. Find $\cos\frac{5\pi}{4}$.
7. Find $\tan(\frac{\pi}{6})$.
8. Find $\sec(\frac{\pi}{2})$.
9. Find $\csc(-\frac{4\pi}{3})$.
10. Find $\cot \pi$.

Inverse Trigonometric Functions

There is an inverse function for each of the six trigonometric functions. Each function is denoted by writing -1 above and to the right of the original trigonometric function, in the same position where we would write an exponent. For example, the inverse sine function is noted by sin⁻¹.

BIG TIME WARNING

The -1 is NOT really an exponent! tan⁻¹ x is NOT $\frac{1}{\tan x}$!

The six inverse trigonometric functions are defined as follows:

sin⁻¹x = the number y in the interval $[-\frac{\pi}{2}, \frac{\pi}{2}]$ such that sin y = x.

cos⁻¹x = the number y in the interval $[0, \pi]$ such that cos y = x.

tan⁻¹x = the number y in the interval $[-\frac{\pi}{2}, \frac{\pi}{2}]$ such that tan y = x.

sec⁻¹x = the number y in the interval $[0, \pi]$ such that sec y = x.

csc⁻¹x = the number y in the interval $[-\frac{\pi}{2}, \frac{\pi}{2}]$ such that csc y = x.

cot⁻¹x = the number y in the interval $[0, \pi]$ such that cot y = x.

Another name for each inverse trigonometric function is the name of the original trigonometric function, with the prefix *arc* attached to the front. For example, the inverse tangent function is also called the arctangent function, and is abbreviated by either *arctan* or *tan⁻¹*.

The possible values for each inverse trigonometric function are chosen so that there is one and only one possible number in the interval which works. If we ask for the arccos of 0.235, for example, I am really asking for a number whose cosine is 0.235. We can add another 2π ; i.e., 360°, to that angle, and we'll get another angle whose cosine is also 0.235. Remember that the one unbreakable rule of functions is: a function must give you the same answer every time the same input is introduced. So mathematicians have decided that the arccos function will always choose the number <u>between 0 and π</u> whose cosine is 0.235. In this case, the number is approximately 1.3336.

Domains of the Inverse Trigonometric Functions

The domain of each inverse trigonometric function is the range of the corresponding trigonometric function. The ranges of the sine and cosine function are both [-1, 1], and so the domains of the sin⁻¹ and cos⁻¹ functions are [-1, 1]. This makes sense because sin⁻¹x is supposed to be a number y whose sine is x. But if x were the number 98.6, for example, there is no number whose sine is 98.6. Therefore sin⁻¹(98.6) cannot exist. The domains of all six inverse trigonometric functions are listed:

Function	Domain
sin⁻¹	[-1, 1]
cos⁻¹	[-1, 1]
tan⁻¹	$(-\infty, \infty)$
sec⁻¹	$(-\infty, -1] \cup [1, \infty)$
csc⁻¹	$(-\infty, -1] \cup [1, \infty)$
cot⁻¹	$(-\infty, \infty)$

For any number x in the domain of the arcsin function, the following identity always holds:

$$\sin(\arcsin x) = x.$$

The same idea works with the other five trigonometric functions. If I apply any inverse trigonometric function to a number in its domain, and then apply the corresponding trigonometric function to the result, I end up back where I started.

•Example:

Find tan(tan⁻¹ 2).

SOLUTION:

Tan⁻¹ 2 is some number y between $-\frac{\pi}{2}$ and $\frac{\pi}{2}$ such that the tangent of y is 2. Therefore, if we take the tangent of y, we obviously get 2! So tan(tan⁻¹ 2) = 2. Note that we never had to figure out the actual value of tan⁻¹ 2 at all.

BIG TIME WARNING

This identity does NOT work in reverse! It is NOT always true that tan⁻¹(tan x) = x. (The same warning applies to the other five functions.) The next example will make that point more clearly.

•Example:

Find sin⁻¹(sin 11.8).

SOLUTION:

I know right away that the answer is NOT 11.8, because $\sin^{-1}x$ is always a number between $-\frac{\pi}{2}$ and $\frac{\pi}{2}$, no matter what x is. And 11.8 is not in that interval. However, sin⁻¹(sin 11.8) is a number whose sine is the sine of 11.8. In other words, we seek a number which has the same sine as 11.8 and which lies in the interval $[-\frac{\pi}{2}, \frac{\pi}{2}]$. Now if we draw an angle of 11.8 radians in standard position, we will find that the terminal side ends in the fourth quadrant, and makes an angle of about 0.7664 radians with the positive x-axis (Two full counterclockwise rotations back to the positive x-axis would be an angle of 4π, or about 12.5664 radians. Therefore 11.8 radians would be about 12.5664 - 11.8 = 0.7664 radians short of the positive x-axis).

So if we rotate clockwise from the x-axis to the terminal side of our 11.8 radian angle, we will have gone through an angle of -0.7664 radians. Therefore 11.8 and -0.7664 have the same sine (because they both have the same terminal side). Furthermore, -0.7664 is in the interval $[-\frac{\pi}{2}, \frac{\pi}{2}]$, so -0.7764 must be the number we want.

sin⁻¹(sin 11.8) = -0.7764

•Example:

Find arccos(cos(-2)).

SOLUTION:

An angle of -2 radians has its terminal side in QIII. The cosine function is negative in the third quadrant. Therefore cos(-2) is negative. Now, the arccos always has to be between 0 and π. The numbers in that interval are all represented by angles in the first and second quadrants. But more precisely, the arccosine of a negative number is represented by a second quadrant angle, because any first quadrant angle has a positive cosine. Therefore we seek an angle in the second quadrant, which has the same cosine as -2. Next, we remember that any two angles with the same reference angle have the same trigonometric function values. So we want a second quadrant angle with the same reference angle as -2. First, we calculate the reference angle, which is about 1.1416. Then

103

we draw a second quadrant angle which has a reference angle of 1.1416. In this case, that angle is π-1.14.6 = 2. The calculations are clarified by this diagram.

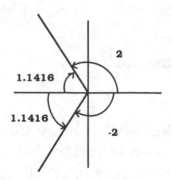

Therefore, arccos(cos(-2)) = 2.

•Example:

Find: a. $\tan(\cos^{-1}(\frac{3}{5}))$
       b. $\sec(\tan^{-1}(-2))$.

SOLUTIONS:

a. $\cos^{-1}(\frac{3}{5})$ is represented by an angle between o and π (i.e., in either the first or second quadrants), whose cosine is $\frac{3}{5}$. Since $\frac{3}{5}$ is a positive number, and angles in the second quadrant have negative cosines, we know $\cos^{-1}(\frac{3}{5})$ is represented by a first quadrant angle, between 0 and $\frac{\pi}{2}$. Although we don't know the exact value of this angle, we can draw a picture of it as part of a right triangle in the first quadrant. For a triangle with an adjacent side of length 3 and a hypotenuse of length 5, the Pythagorean Theorem tells us that the opposite side must have length 4:

$$x^2 + y^2 = r^2$$
$$3^2 + y^2 = 5^2$$
$$y^2 = 25 - 9 = 16$$
$$y = 4$$

Looking at the diagram, we can see that the tangent of $\cos^{-1}(\frac{3}{5})$ is equal to $\frac{4}{3}$.

b. Using logic similar to that in Part a, we conclude that $\tan^{-1}(-2)$ is represented by an angle in the fourth quadrant, and that the angle can be drawn as part of the right triangle in the following diagram:

104

$$r^2 = x^2 + y^2 = 1 + 4$$
$$r = \sqrt{5}$$

From the diagram, we can see that the secant of $\tan^{-1}(-2) = \frac{r}{x} = \frac{\sqrt{5}}{1}$ or $\sqrt{5}$.

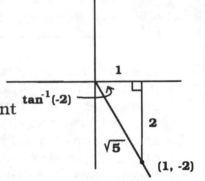

Using a Calculator to Find Inverse Trigonometric Functions

Almost any calculator which has trigonometric functions also has the inverse trigonometric functions. Not all calculators work the same way, but the most common method for getting an inverse sine, cosine, or tangent on a calculator is:

1. Make sure the calculator is in Radian mode.
2. Enter the number whose inverse trigonometric function you want.
3. Press the INV or 2ND key, usually toward the top left-hand of the keyboard.
4. Press the key for the trigonometric function corresponding to the inverse function you want. If you press the cosine key, for example, you will get the arccosine of the original number which you entered in Step 2.

NOTE: If you want the inverse of the secant, cosecant, or cotangent functions, then enter the *reciprocal* of the number you are interested in when performing Step 2. Then, for Step 4, press the reciprocal function for the one you are interested in. For example, if you want the inverse secant, press the cosine in Step 4.

SECOND NOTE: If you perform Step 2 through 4, but with your calculator in degree mode, you will get the number of degrees corresponding to the radian measure which you get by doing the process as described with the calculator in Radian mode. However, the mathematical functions $\sin^{-1}$, $\cos^{-1}$, etc., do not have two different modes. We *always* assume radians!

Trigonometric Functions, Exercise 3. Inverse Trigonometric Functions.

1. $\tan(\tan^{-1} 3)$
2. $\sin(\sin^{-1} 2)$
3. $\sin^{-1}(\frac{1}{\sqrt{2}})$
4. $\cos^{-1}(-\frac{1}{\sqrt{2}})$
5. $\sin^{-1}(-\frac{1}{\sqrt{2}})$
6. $\cos(\arcsin \frac{3}{5})$
7. $\sin(\arcsin \frac{3}{5})$
8. $\tan(\sin^{-1} 0)$
9. $\arccos(\sin \frac{\pi}{2})$
10. $\sec(\tan^{-1}(-\frac{4}{5}))$

The graphs of the trigonometric functions are different from the graphs of polynomials or rational functions in one very important respect: If you travel along the graph from left to right, you will find that the graph repeats itself over and over again. This happens because the trigonometric functions of an angle go through the same values every time we rotate the terminal side of the angle through an additional 2π (360°). Functions which repeat themselves like this are called **periodic** functions. All six trigonometric functions are periodic.

The **period** of a trigonometric function is the smallest interval over which it always repeats itself. For example, we know that all six trigonometric functions repeat after each interval of 2π, but it happens that the tangent and cotangent functions actually repeat themselves over an interval of just π. So the periods of the sine, cosine, secant, and cosecant functions are all 2π, and the periods of the tangent and cotangent functions are π.

Having a periodic function is an advantage for graphing. All we need to know is what the graph looks like through one cycle (a cycle is the interval of one period on the graph), and we just simply repeat it forever to the left and right.

The graphs of the six trigonometric functions are shown below:

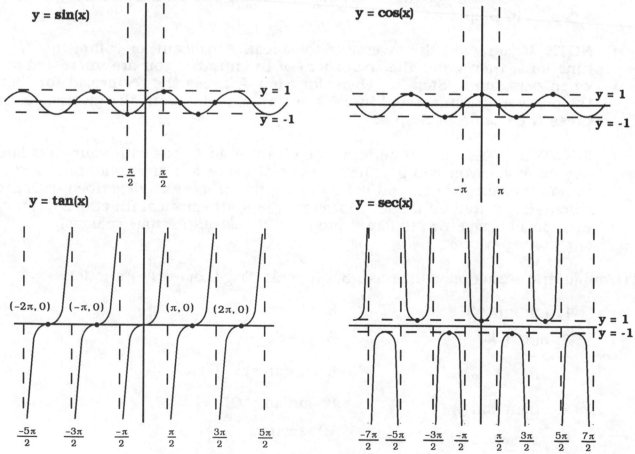

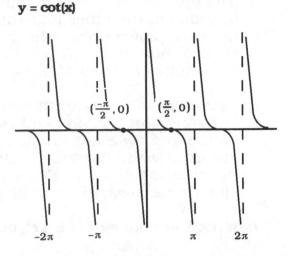

y = csc(x)

y = 1
y = -1

-4π -3π -2π -π π 2π 3π 4π

y = cot(x)

$(\frac{-\pi}{2}, 0)$ $(\frac{\pi}{2}, 0)$

-2π -π π 2π

The graphs illustrate several properties of the trigonometric functions:

1. As mentioned above, the tangent and cotangent functions have a period of π, and the sine, cosine, secant, and cosecant functions have a period of 2π.

   We can figure the period of a function by taking any convenient point on the graph to be the beginning of a period, looking for the corresponding point in the next cycle to the right, and then calculating the difference between the x-coordinates of the two points. The graph of the secant function is shown here as an example:

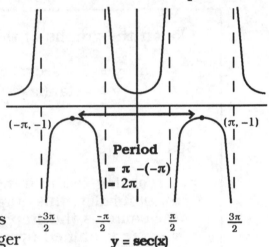

$(-\pi, -1)$ $(\pi, -1)$

Period
$= \pi - (-\pi)$
$= 2\pi$

$\frac{-3\pi}{2}$ $\frac{-\pi}{2}$ $\frac{\pi}{2}$ $\frac{3\pi}{2}$

y = sec(x)

2. The graphs of the tangent and secant functions have asymptotes at all x values of the form $\frac{n\pi}{2}$, where n is an odd integer (positive or negative). The graphs of the cotangent and cosecant functions have asymptotes at all integer multiples of π. These asymptotes are a consequence of the definitions of the functions in terms of x, y, and r for angles in standard position. For example, the cotangent of an angle whose terminal side contains the point (x, y) is $\frac{x}{y}$. Therefore, there will be an asymptote for any angle for which y = 0 on the terminal side of the angle. That happens only when the terminal side of the angle is the positive or negative x-axis. The only such angles are the integer multiples of π. Therefore, we expect asymptotes of the graph of the cotangent function to occur at all the integer multiples of π.

BIG TIME WARNING

Do not confuse the x- and y-coordinates associated with an angle in standard position with the x- and y-coordinates of a point on the graph of a trigonometric function.

---

3. The domains of the sine and cosine functions are all real numbers. The domains of the other four functions are all numbers except those where the asymptotes occur. In this respect those four functions work like rational functions. Remember that the domain of a function is the set of all x values covered by its graph (from left to right).

4. The range of the tangent and cotangent functions are all real numbers. The ranges of the sine and cosine functions are [-1, 1]. The ranges of the secant and cosecant functions are $(-\infty, -1] \cup [1, \infty)$. Note that these ranges are exactly the domains of the corresponding inverse functions defined in the previous section. Remember that the range of a function is the set of all y values covered by its graph (up and down).

Modified Versions of the Trigonometric Graphs

The rules of graph transformations given in Chapter 5 apply, of course, to the graphs of the trigonometric functions.

•Examples:

Sketch the graphs of the following:

    a. $y = 3 + \sec x$
    b. $y = -2\tan(x + \frac{\pi}{2})$.

SOLUTIONS

a. According to the transformation rules, this graph is the same as the graph of $y = \sec x$, shifted upward by 3 units:

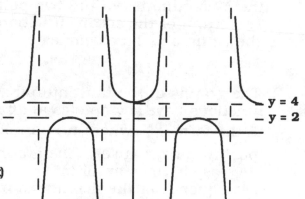

$y = 3 + \sec(x)$

b. The transformation rules in this case say that we start with the graph of $y = \tan x$, shift to the left by $\frac{\pi}{2}$, reflect in the x-axis (up and down), and stretch the graph vertically by a factor of 2:

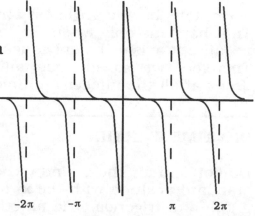

$y = -2\tan(x + \frac{\pi}{2})$

108

Variations on the Graphs of the Sine and Cosine Functions

The periodic wave form of the sine and cosine graphs (called, not surprisingly, a *sine wave*) has many applications in science and engineering. Graphs of various forms of the sine and cosine functions are used so frequently that specific terminology has been established to describe any graph based on the sine or cosine functions. The terminology is:

Horizontal axis: the horizontal straight line through the center of the wave. For the unmodified sine and cosine graphs, the horizontal axis is the x-axis (i.e., the line y = 0).

Amplitude: the vertical distance between the horizontal axis and the *peak* at the top of each wave cycle. For the unmodified sine and cosine graphs, the amplitude is 1, because the peaks all have a y-coordinate of 1, and the horizontal axis has a y-coordinate of 0.

Phase shift: the horizontal distance (left or right) by which the graph is shifted from the original position of the graph of y = sin x or y = cos x. In the case of a sine graph, the phase shift is applied to the point at the origin where the graph crosses the horizontal axis. In the case of a cosine graph, the phase shift is applied to the peak at the point (0, 1).

Calculating the Period, Horizontal Axis, Amplitude, and Phase Shift

If we are trying to graph an equation of the form

$$y = A + B\sin(Cx + D)$$
$$\text{or}$$
$$y = A + B\cos(Cx + D)$$

we can calculate the four important parameters by using the following formulas:

period = $\frac{2\pi}{C}$

horizontal axis: y = A

phase shift = $\frac{-D}{C}$ The shift is to the left if the number is negative, and to the right if the number is positive.

amplitude = $|B|$

One more rule which affects graphs of modified sine and cosine functions is:

If B is negative, then the graph must be reflected in the x-axis (up and down). All the peaks become valleys, and all the valleys become peaks. This rule is merely a special case of the graph transformation rule in Chapter 5. That rule stated: a minus sign in front of a function causes a reflection of the graph in the x-axis.

•Example:

Sketch the graphs of the following functions, using the information provided by calculating the amplitude, period, horizontal axis, and phase shift.

    a. $y = -1 + 2\sin(x - \frac{2}{3})$

    b. $y = 2 - 3\cos(2x + \frac{\pi}{3})$

SOLUTIONS

a. According to the formulas above, we have A = -1, B = 2, C = 1, and D = $-\frac{2}{3}$. Therefore:

amplitude:	$\lvert 2 \rvert = 2$	
period:	$\frac{2\pi}{1} = 2\pi$	
horizontal axis:	$y = -1$	(i.e., y = A)
phase shift	$\frac{-(-\frac{2}{3})}{1} = \frac{2}{3}$	The shift will be to the right because the number is positive.

Since the horizontal axis is y = -1, and the amplitude is 2, the peaks of the waves will be 2 units above the line y = -1, which means the peaks will have a y-coordinate of -1 + 2 = 1. The low points will be 2 units below the line y = -1, which means they will have a y-coordinate of -1 - 2 = -3. Since the period is 2π. the peaks (and valleys) will be horizontally spaced 2π units from each other.

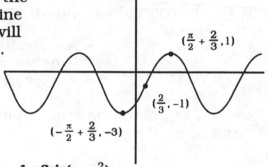

$y = -1 + 2\sin(x - \frac{2}{3})$

Finally, the phase shift of $\frac{2}{3}$ means that the point at the origin, where the original sine graph intersects the horizontal axis, will now be shifted $\frac{2}{3}$ units to the right.

b. Using the values A = 2, B = -3, C = 2, and D = $\frac{\pi}{3}$, we get:

amplitude:	3
period:	π
horizontal axis:	y = 2
phase shift:	$\frac{-\pi}{6}$, or about 0.5236 units to the left.

110

Using the calculated values, we see that the peaks of the graph will have y-coordinates of 2 + 3 = 5, and the valleys will have y-coordinates of 2 - 3 = -1. The horizontal distances between consecutive peaks will be equal to the period π, or about 3.1416. The peak which intercepts the y-axis at the point (0, 1) in the graph of y = cos x, will be moved to the left by $\frac{\pi}{6}$ units. Finally, since B = -3 is negative, we reflect the graph vertically so that the peaks become valleys and the valleys become peaks.

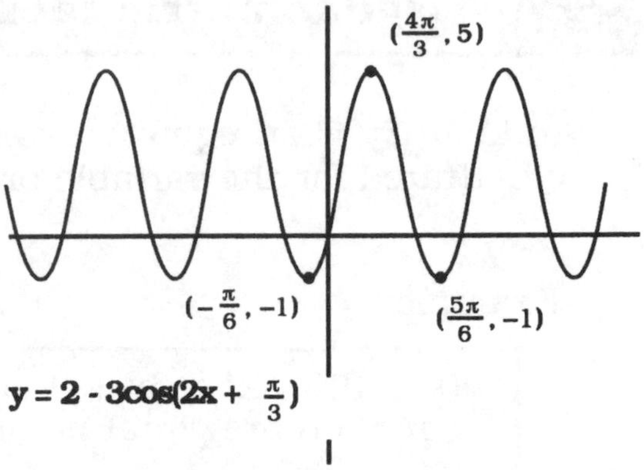

$(\frac{4\pi}{3}, 5)$

$(-\frac{\pi}{6}, -1)$

$(\frac{5\pi}{6}, -1)$

$y = 2 - 3\cos(2x + \frac{\pi}{3})$

Trigonometric Functions, Exercise 4. Graphs of Trigonometric Functions.

Sketch the graphs of the following functions:

1. $\tan(x - \frac{\pi}{3})$

2. $-\tan(x - \frac{\pi}{3})$

3. $\frac{1}{2}\sec x$

4. $\frac{1}{2}\sec(x + \frac{\pi}{2})$

5. $3\csc x$

6. $2 + 3\csc x$

7. $\cot(x + \frac{\pi}{2})$

8. $-\cot(x + \frac{\pi}{2})$

9. $2 + \sin(x - \pi)$

10. $2 - \sin(3x + \frac{3\pi}{2})$

11. $1 + \cos(2x)$

12. $1 - 3\cos(2x)$

An **identity** is an equation which is true regardless of the value substituted for the variable or variables in the equation.

•Example:

> $(x + 3)^2 = x^2 + 6x + 9$ is an identity, because the two sides of the equation are equal no matter what value is substituted for x.

In the first section of this chapter, we learned that the secant, cosecant, and cotangent functions can be expressed as the reciprocals of the cosine, sine, and tangent functions respectively. Because all six functions are defined in terms of the three numbers x, y, and r, and since r is related to x and y by the equation r= $\sqrt{x^2 + y^2}$, we can find several useful identities which relate the six trigonometic functions. It is a fact that if A stands for <u>any</u> number, or <u>any</u> angle expressed in radians, or <u>any</u> angle expressed in degrees, the following identities are true:

$$\tan A = \frac{\sin A}{\cos A}$$

$$\cot A = \frac{\cos A}{\sin A}$$

$$\sin^2 A + \cos^2 A = 1 \qquad \text{Remember that } \sin^2 A \text{ means } (\sin A)^2.$$

$$\tan^2 A + 1 = \sec^2 A$$

$$\cot^2 A + 1 = \csc^2 A$$

As examples, we show the derivations of two of the given identities. If the point (x, y) is on the terminal side of angle A, and r is defined as usual as $\sqrt{x^2 + y^2}$ then:

$$\frac{\sin A}{\cos A} = \frac{\frac{y}{r}}{\frac{x}{r}} = \frac{y}{x} = \tan A. \text{ Hence, } \tan A = \frac{\sin A}{\cos A}.$$

$$\text{Also, } \cot^2 A + 1 \quad = \frac{x^2}{y^2} + 1 = \frac{x^2}{y^2} + \frac{y^2}{y^2} = \frac{x^2 + y^2}{y^2}$$

$$= \frac{r^2}{y^2} = \left(\frac{r}{y}\right)^2 = \csc^2 A.$$

In addition, we have the following *reciprocal identities*, which were noted when the secant, cosecant, and cotangent functions were first defined:

$$\sec A = \frac{1}{\cos A} \qquad\qquad \cos A = \frac{1}{\sec A}$$

$$\csc A = \frac{1}{\sin A} \qquad\qquad \sin A = \frac{1}{\csc A}$$

$$\cot A = \frac{1}{\tan A} \qquad\qquad \tan A = \frac{1}{\cot A}$$

The identities are useful in simplifying complicated trigonometric expressions. For one thing, they enable us to express any trigonometric function in terms of the sine and cosine:

•Example:

Simplify the expression $\frac{\tan x + \sin x}{1 + \sec x}$ by expressing every trigonometric function in terms of the sine and cosine of x, and then simplifying algebraically.

SOLUTION:

$$\frac{\tan x + \sin x}{1 + \sec x} = \frac{\frac{\sin x}{\cos x} + \sin x}{1 + \frac{1}{\cos x}} = \frac{\sin x + \sin x \cos x}{\cos x + 1}$$

(We get this last one by multiplying both the top and bottom of the fraction by cos x.)

But this $= \frac{\sin x\,(1 + \cos x)}{\cos x + 1} = \sin x$, by dividing the $1 + \cos x$ out of both the top and bottom.

Therefore $\frac{\tan x + \sin x}{1 + \sec x} = \sin x$ for <u>any</u> value of x for which the expression is defined.

Sometimes the simplification procedure does not involve expressing everything in terms of sines and cosines. There is no formal step-by-step method which works for all simplification problems. However, several ideas come up again and again, and are therefore worth remembering:

1. Each of the identities above has several variations which are obtainable by manipulating the equation. For example,

$$\tan A = \frac{\sin A}{\cos A} \longrightarrow \tan A \cos A = \sin A$$

$$\cot^2 + 1 = \csc^2 A \longrightarrow \cot^2 A - \csc^2 = -1$$

This idea can be used for the following simplification:

$$\frac{\sec^2 x - 1}{1 - \csc^2 x} = \frac{\tan^2 x}{-\cot^2 x} = \frac{\tan^2 x}{-\frac{1}{\tan^2 x}} = \frac{\tan^2 x}{-1}(\tan^2 x) = -\tan^4 x$$

2. Several of the identities, in some form, give us the difference of two squares, which can then be factored:

$$\frac{\sin^2 x}{\cos x + 1} = \frac{1 - \cos^2 x}{\cos x + 1} = \frac{(1 - \cos x)(1 + \cos x)}{1 + \cos x} = 1 - \cos x$$

3. A fraction with more than one term in the numerator, but only one term in the denominator, can be split into a sum of fractions, each having a single term in the numerator. The resulting simpler fractions can then sometimes be simplified individually:

$$\frac{\sec y + \csc y}{\sec y \csc y} = \frac{\sec y}{\sec y \csc y} + \frac{\csc y}{\sec y \csc y}$$

$$= \frac{1}{\csc y} + \frac{1}{\sec y} = \sin y + \cos y$$

4. Factoring out a common expression often leads to simplification:

$$\sec A + \frac{\sec A \sin^2 A}{\cos^2 A} = \sec A(1 + \frac{\sin^2 A}{\cos^2 A})$$

$$= \sec A(1 + \tan^2 A) = \sec A(\sec^2 A) = \sec^3 A$$

5. If we have a fraction within a fraction, we can simplify by multiplying the top and bottom of the big fraction by the denominator of the smaller fraction which we want to be rid of:

$$\frac{\sec x + 1}{\sec x - \cos x} = \frac{\frac{1}{\cos x} + 1}{\frac{1}{\cos x} - \cos x}\left(\frac{\cos x}{\cos x}\right) = \frac{1 + \cos x}{1 - \cos^2 x}$$

$$= \frac{1 + \cos x}{(1 + \cos x)(1 - \cos x)} = \frac{1}{1 - \cos x}$$

6. Perfect squares, of the form $(a + b)^2 = a^2 + 2ab + b^2$, occur commonly:

$$\frac{\cos^4 x - 2\csc^2 x + 1}{\cos^4 x} = \frac{(\cos^2 x - 1)^2}{\cos^4 x} = \frac{(-\sin^2 x)^2}{(\cos^2 x)^2}$$

$$= (-\tan^2 x)^2 = \tan^4 x$$

7. As already mentioned, every trigonometric function can be expressed in terms of sines and cosines.

Trigonometric Functions, Exercise 5. Trigonometric Identities.

Simplify each expression.

1. $\csc x - \cos x \cot x$

2. $\sec x - \sin x \tan x$

3. $\frac{1 + \tan B}{1 - \tan B} + \frac{1 + \cot B}{1 - \cot B}$

4. $\frac{\sin y \tan y}{\cos y}$

5. $\frac{\cos A}{\sin A \cot A}$

6. $\frac{\tan^2 x + 1}{\sec x}$

7. $\frac{\sin^4 x - \cos^4 x}{\sin^2 x - \cos^2 x}$

8. $\frac{1}{1 - \sin A} + \frac{1}{1 + \sin A}$

9. $1 - \frac{\sin^2 x}{1 - \cos x}$

10. $\tan y + \frac{\cos y}{1 + \sin y}$

114

Multiple and Half Angle Formulas

As mentioned earlier, the parentheses in trigonometric expressions do not stand for multiplication: cos(x+y) means we are applying the cosine function to the quantity x+y; we are NOT multiplying cos TIMES x+y! In particular, cos(x+y) is not equal to cos(x) + cos(y).

•Example:

Use a calculator to find:

      a. cos 1
      b. cos 3
      c. cos 1 + cos 3
      d. cos(1+3); in other words, cos 4.

SOLUTION:

a. cos 1 = 0.5403
b. cos 3 = -0.98999
c. cos 1 + cos 3 = sum of the answers from a and b = -0.44969
d. cos 4 = -0.65364

Since the answers to c and d are different, we know that the cos(1+3) is not equal to cos 1 + cos 3.

Trigonometric functions do not "distribute" across sums of numbers. But there are formulas to tell us how to find the values of the trigonometric functions of the sum or difference of two angles, if we know the values of the trigonometric functions of the individual numbers in the sum or difference. The formulas for sine, consine, and tangent are given below:

$$\sin(A+B) = \sin A \cos B + \sin B \cos A$$

$$\sin(A-B) = \sin A \cos B - \sin B \cos A$$

$$\cos(A+B) = \cos A \cos B - \sin A \sin B$$

$$\cos(A-B) = \cos A \cos B + \sin A \sin B$$

$$\tan(A + B) = \frac{\tan A + \tan B}{1 - \tan A \tan B}$$

$$\tan(A - B) = \frac{\tan A - \tan B}{1 + \tan A \tan B}$$

These formulas are valid whether A and B are real numbers, angles expressed in degrees or angles expressed in radians.

The derivations of these formulas are based on geometric arguments and can be found in most trigonometry textbooks. There are also formulas for finding the values of the trigonometric functions of 2x and $\frac{1}{2}$x if we know the values of the trigonometric functions of x itself. The formulas for 2x are derived easily form the formulas for A + B if we just let x = A = B. The formulas are:

$$\sin 2x = 2\sin x \cos x$$

$$\cos 2x = \cos^2 x - \sin^2 x$$

$$\sin(\tfrac{1}{2}x) = \pm\sqrt{\tfrac{1-\cos x}{2}}$$

$$\cos(\tfrac{1}{2}x) = \pm\sqrt{\tfrac{1+\cos x}{2}}$$

$$\tan(\tfrac{1}{2}x) = \tfrac{\sin x}{1+\cos x}$$

BIG TIME WARNING

sin 2x is NOT the same as 2sin x! For example, if $x = \frac{\pi}{2}$, then sin 2x = sin π = 0, but 2sin x = 2sin$\frac{\pi}{2}$= 2(1) = 2. The same principle applies to all of the formulas above.

•Example:

Find:
   a. sin 15°
   b. cos$\frac{7\pi}{12}$

SOLUTIONS

a. 15° = 45° - 30°. Since we know the trigonometric function values for 45° and 30°, we can calculate:

$$\sin 15° = \sin 45° \cos 30° - \sin 30° \cos 45°$$
$$= (\tfrac{1}{\sqrt{2}})(\tfrac{\sqrt{3}}{2}) - (\tfrac{1}{2})(\tfrac{1}{\sqrt{2}}) = \tfrac{\sqrt{3}-1}{2\sqrt{2}}, \text{ or } \tfrac{\sqrt{6}-\sqrt{2}}{4}$$

b. $\frac{7\pi}{12} = \frac{\pi}{4} + \frac{\pi}{3}$, so we can calculate cos$\frac{7\pi}{12}$ in terms of the sine and cosine of $\frac{\pi}{4}$ and $\frac{\pi}{3}$:

$$\cos \tfrac{7\pi}{12} = \cos(\tfrac{\pi}{4} + \tfrac{\pi}{3}) = \cos \tfrac{\pi}{4} \cos \tfrac{\pi}{3} - \sin \tfrac{\pi}{4} \sin \tfrac{\pi}{3}$$
$$= (\tfrac{1}{\sqrt{2}})(\tfrac{1}{2}) - (\tfrac{1}{\sqrt{2}})(\tfrac{\sqrt{3}}{2}) = \tfrac{1-\sqrt{3}}{2\sqrt{2}}, \text{ or } \tfrac{\sqrt{2}-\sqrt{6}}{4}.$$

•Example:

Let: A = a first quadrant angle whose sine is $\frac{2}{7}$.

B = a fourth quadrant angle whose tangent is $-\frac{3}{5}$.

Find: (1.) tan(A-B)

(2.) sin(A+B)

SOLUTIONS

(1.) $\tan(A-B) = \frac{\tan A - \tan B}{1 + \tan A \tan B}$ so we need tanA (we already know

$\tan B = -\frac{3}{5}$). The reference angle for A is contained in this
triangle:

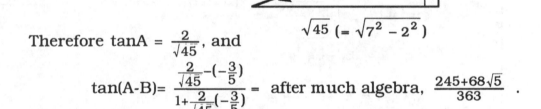

Reference angle for A   7   2

$\sqrt{45}\ (= \sqrt{7^2 - 2^2}\ )$

Therefore $\tan A = \frac{2}{\sqrt{45}}$, and

$\tan(A-B) = \dfrac{\frac{2}{\sqrt{45}} - (-\frac{3}{5})}{1 + \frac{2}{\sqrt{45}}(-\frac{3}{5})}$ = after much algebra, $\frac{245 + 68\sqrt{5}}{363}$.

(2.) sin(A+B) = sinA cosB + sinB cosA. We know sinA, can get cosA
from the diagram in Part 1, and can get sinB and cosB from this
diagram:

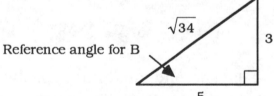

$\sqrt{34}$ 3

Reference angle for B

5

Since B is in QIV, sinB is negative and cosB is positive.

So: $\sin B = \frac{-3}{\sqrt{34}}$

$\cos B = \frac{5}{\sqrt{34}}$

$\sin(A+B) = (\frac{2}{7})(\frac{5}{\sqrt{34}}) + (\frac{-3}{\sqrt{34}})(\frac{\sqrt{45}}{7})$

$= \frac{10 - 3\sqrt{45}}{7\sqrt{34}}$, or $\frac{10\sqrt{34} - 9\sqrt{170}}{238}$

•Example:

Let: $\sin A = \frac{-5}{6}$.

$\pi \le A \le \frac{3\pi}{2}$.

Find: All 6 trigonometric function values for $\frac{A}{2}$.

SOLUTION

In order to use the half-angle formulas from page 116,
we will need sinA (which we already know), and cosA.
Since A is a QIII angle, we know cosA is negative.
The reference angle for A is contained in this triangle:
So $\cos A = -\frac{\sqrt{11}}{6}$.

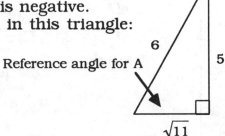

Reference angle for A

6

5

$\sqrt{11}$

Our formulas give:

$$\sin(\tfrac{A}{2}) = \pm\sqrt{\frac{1-\cos A}{2}} = \pm\sqrt{\frac{1-(-\frac{\sqrt{11}}{6})}{2}}$$

$$= \pm\sqrt{\frac{6+\sqrt{11}}{12}}$$

$$\cos(\tfrac{A}{2}) = \pm\sqrt{\frac{1+\cos A}{2}} = \pm\sqrt{\frac{6-\sqrt{11}}{12}}$$

$$\tan(\tfrac{A}{2}) = \frac{\sin A}{1+\cos A} = \frac{-\frac{5}{6}}{1-\frac{\sqrt{11}}{6}} = \frac{-5}{6-\sqrt{11}}$$

We can decide whether to use + or - for the sine and cosine by the
inequality:

$$\pi \le A \le \frac{3\pi}{2} \text{ , so } \frac{\pi}{2} \le \frac{A}{2} \le \frac{3\pi}{4}.$$

Therefore $\frac{A}{2}$ is a second quadrant angle, whose sine is positive, and
tangent and cosine negative. We can find the values of the secant,
cosecant, and cotangent by taking reciprocals. So we have, at last:

$$\sin(\tfrac{A}{2}) = \sqrt{\frac{6+\sqrt{11}}{12}}$$

$$\cos(\tfrac{A}{2}) = -\sqrt{\frac{6-\sqrt{11}}{12}}$$

$$\tan(\tfrac{A}{2}) = \frac{-5}{6-\sqrt{11}}$$

$$\sec(\tfrac{A}{2}) = -\sqrt{\frac{12}{6-\sqrt{11}}}$$

$$\csc(\tfrac{A}{2}) = \sqrt{\frac{12}{6+\sqrt{11}}}$$

$$\cot(\tfrac{A}{2}) = \frac{6-\sqrt{11}}{-5} = \frac{\sqrt{11}-6}{5}$$

•Example:

Use the formula for the difference of two angles to simplify:

a. sin(-x)
b. cos(-x)
c. tan(-x)

SOLUTION

a. sin(-x) = sin(0-x)
            = sin0 cosx - sinx cos0
            = (0)cosx-sinx(1)
            = -sinx

b. cos(-x) = cos(0-x)
            = cos0 cosx + sin0 sinx
            = (1)cosx + (0)sinx
            = cosx

c. tan(-x) =tan(0-x)

$$= \frac{\tan 0 - \tan x}{1 + \tan 0 \tan x}$$

$$= \frac{0 - \tan x}{1 + 0(\tan x)}$$

$$= -\tan x$$

Note that this example shows that the sine and tangent functions are odd functions, and the cosine is an even function. (This can also be verified by looking at the graphs of these functions.)

•Example:

Simplify $\frac{1-\tan^2 y}{1+\tan^2 y}$.

SOLUTION

$$\frac{1-\tan^2 y}{1+\tan^2 y} = \frac{1-\frac{\sin^2 y}{\cos^2 y}}{\sec^2 y}$$

$$= \frac{1-\frac{\sin^2 y}{\cos^2 y}}{\frac{1}{\cos^2 y}} \left(\frac{\cos^2 y}{\cos^2 y} \right)$$

$$= \frac{\cos^2 y - \sin^2 y}{1} = \cos^2 y - \sin^2 y = \cos 2y$$

Trigonometric Functions, Exercise 6. Multiple and Half Angle Formulas.

1. Find tan 15°, using $15° = (\frac{1}{2})(30°)$.
2. Find $\sin\frac{5\pi}{12}$, using $\frac{5\pi}{12} = \frac{\pi}{4} + \frac{\pi}{6}$.
3. Find cos 165°, using $165° = 225° - 60°$.

For problems 4 - 7, use the following facts about angles A and B.

$$-\frac{3\pi}{2} \le A \le -\pi$$

B is in QIII

The reference angles for A and B are shown in the following triangles:

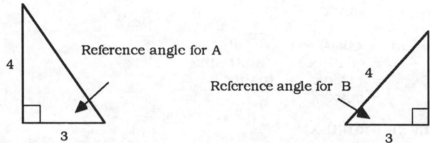

Reference angle for A

Reference angle for B

4. Find sin(A+B).
5. Find $\cos(\frac{A}{2})$.
6. Find tan(A-B).
7. Find sec2A.
8. Simplify sin(x-π).
9. Simplify $\cos(\frac{\pi}{2} - x)$.
10. Simplify tan(x+π).
11. Simplify $2\cos^2 A - 1$.
12. Simplify $\frac{1+\cos 2y}{\sin^2 y}$.

Part 7 Solving Trigonometric Equations

A trigonometric equation is an equation in which the unknown is part of one or more trigonometric functions. The simplest trigonometric equation is one which simply states that some trigonometric function is equal to a given number.

•Example:

Solve the equation sin x = -.055, given $\pi \le x \le 2\pi$.

120

SOLUTION:

We can use a calculator and the inverse sine function to learn that -0.58236 is a number whose sine is -0.55. Now, -0.58236 is not within the specified range of π to 2π, and so -0.58236 cannot be the solution to the equation. However, the specified range does require an angle in the third or fourth quadrant, and -0.58236 is in the fourth quadrant. All we need is the angle in the interval [π, 2π], which is coterminal with an angle of -0.58236 radians. Therefore -0.58236 + 2π = 5.70082 fits the requirements. It is the solution to the equation.

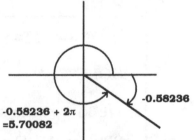

•Example:

Describe <u>all</u> solutions to the equation sin x = -0.55.

SOLUTION:

From the example above, we know that 5.70082 is one solution to the equation and that 5.70082 is represented by a fourth quadrant angle. The sine function is negative in the third quadrant as well, and therefore there is a third quadrant angle whose sine is also -0.55. That angle must have the same reference angle as 5.70082, which is 0.58236. The third quadrant angle with a reference angle of 0.58236 is π + 0.58236 = 3.72396.

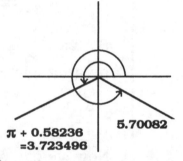

The two solutions we have found (5.70082 and 3.72396) are the only two solutions in the interval [0, 2π], since the sine function is negative only in the third and fourth quadrants. Therefore, any other solution to the equation will have to be represented by an angle which is coterminal with either 5.70082 or 3.72396. Stated another way: any solution must either be either 5.70082 or 3.72396, plus some integer multiple of 2π. To express mathematically, use the letter n to represent an arbitary integer, and to say that the general solution to the equation sin x = -.55 is:

$$5.70082 + 2n\pi$$
$$\text{and}$$
$$3.72396 + 2n\pi.$$

If the trigonometric function in an equation is applied to a more complicated expression involving x, we first solve as if the more complicated expression were itself the unknown. We then we set the expression equal to each solution and solve algebraically for x.

•Example:

> Solve the equation $\sin(2x - \frac{\pi}{3}) = 0.5$, with $-\pi \leq x \leq \pi$.
>
> SOLUTION
>
> We know that the angles between 0 and 2π whose sines are 0.5 are $\frac{\pi}{6}$ and $\frac{5\pi}{6}$, so $2x - \frac{\pi}{3}$ will have to be represented by an angle which is coterminal with one of those two angles. The inequality given with the problem tells us in what range x must be, but not where the legal values for $2x - \frac{\pi}{3}$ are. But we can find those easily by solving the given inequality for $2x - \frac{\pi}{3}$:
>
> $$-\pi \leq x \leq \pi$$
> $$-2\pi \leq 2x \leq 2\pi$$
> $$-2\pi - \frac{\pi}{3} \leq 2x - \frac{\pi}{3} \leq 2\pi - \frac{\pi}{3}$$
> $$-\frac{7\pi}{3} \leq 2x - \frac{\pi}{3} \leq \frac{5\pi}{3}$$
>
> So $2x - \frac{\pi}{3}$ must live in the interval $[-\frac{7\pi}{3}, \frac{5\pi}{3}]$, and be represented by an angle coterminal with either $\frac{\pi}{6}$ or $\frac{5\pi}{6}$. The possibilities are $\frac{-11\pi}{6}$, $\frac{-7\pi}{6}$, $\frac{\pi}{6}$ and $\frac{5\pi}{6}$.
>
> Now we can solve the four equations for x:
>
> $$2x - \frac{\pi}{3} = \frac{-11\pi}{6} \longrightarrow x = \frac{-3\pi}{4}$$
> $$2x - \frac{\pi}{3} = \frac{-7\pi}{6} \longrightarrow x = \frac{-5\pi}{12}$$
> $$2x - \frac{\pi}{3} = \frac{\pi}{6} \longrightarrow x = \frac{\pi}{4}$$
> $$2x - \frac{\pi}{3} = \frac{5\pi}{6} \longrightarrow x = \frac{7\pi}{12}$$
>
> The result yields four solutions to the original equation.

If the equation has an algebraic expression involving trigonometric functions, we must simplify the equation algebraically until we get one or more simpler equations of the kind we have already shown above.

•Example:

Solve: $\sin x \tan x + \sin x = \frac{1}{2}(\tan x + 1)$, with $90° \le x \le 180°$.

SOLUTION:

If we factor the left-hand side we get:
$$\sin x(\tan x + 1) = \frac{1}{2}(\tan x + 1).$$
At this point WE DO NOT DIVIDE BOTH SIDES BY TAN X + 1!!! Doing that would eliminate any solution in which tan x + 1 = 0. The correct procedure is to subtract $\frac{1}{2}(\tan x + 1)$ from both sides, and then factor the left-hand side by grouping:
$$\sin x(\tan x + 1) - \frac{1}{2}(\tan x + 1) = 0$$
$$(\sin x - \frac{1}{2})(\tan x + 1) = 0$$
Now we have a traditional rule: If the product of two factors equals zero, we set each factor equal to zero separately and solve.
In each case there is only one solution in the given interval [90°, 180°]. Since the interval is given in degrees, that means the answer is desired in degrees:

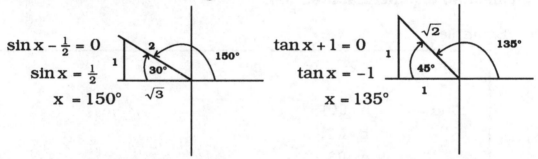

$\sin x - \frac{1}{2} = 0$

$\sin x = \frac{1}{2}$

$x = 150°$

$\tan x + 1 = 0$

$\tan x = -1$

$x = 135°$

Trigonometric Functions, Exercise 7. Solving Trigonometric Equations.

Solve:

1. $\sec x = 2$ $-\pi \le x \le \pi$

2. $\sec^2 x = 4$ $-\pi \le x \le \pi$

3. $\sec(x + 60°) = 2$ $0 < x \le 360°$

4. $\tan(2x) = \sqrt{3}$ $0 \le x < 2\pi$

5. $\tan x \cos x + 1 = \tan x + \cos x$ $-180° < x \le 180°$

6. $\cos x + 82 = 83$ $0 < x < \pi$

7. $\cos x + 83 = 82$ $0 < x \le \pi$

8. $\sin x + 83 = 85$ $-360° < x < 360°$

9. $\sin x \tan x + 2 \tan x = 0$ $-\pi \le x \le \pi$

10. $\cot^2 x + 2\cot x - 3 = 0$ $0 < x \le 360°$

11. $\sin^2 x = 1$ (general solution in radians)

12. $\tan^2(-x) = \frac{3}{4}$ (general solution in degrees)

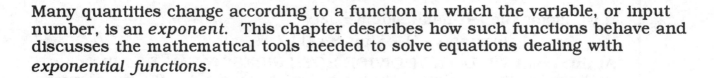

Exponential and Logarithmic Functions

Many quantities change according to a function in which the variable, or input number, is an *exponent*. This chapter describes how such functions behave and discusses the mathematical tools needed to solve equations dealing with *exponential functions*.

Part 1 | **Exponential Functions**

The function

$$f(x) = 3^x$$

is a function into which we can substitute any real number for x —i.e., the domain of the function is all real numbers. A function such as this, in which the variable designating the input number is part or all of the exponent, is called an **exponential function**.

•Example:

Let: $f(x) = 3^x$.

Find: a. f(0)
b. f(1)
c. f(3)
d. f(-2)
e. f(0.5)
f. f(1.6)

SOLUTION

a. $f(0) = 3^0 = 1$
b. $f(1) = 3^1 = 3$
c. $f(3) = 3^3 = 27$
d. $f(-2) = 3^{-2} = \frac{1}{9}$
e. $f(0.5) = 3^{0.5}$

$$= 3^{\frac{1}{2}}$$

$$= \sqrt{3}$$

$$\approx 1.7320508$$

$$f.\ f(1.6)\ =\ 3^{1.6}$$

$$=\ 3^{\frac{16}{10}}$$

$$=\ \left(\sqrt[10]{3}\right)^{16}$$

$$\approx\ 5.7995461$$

Here is the graph of the function $f(x) = 3^x$.

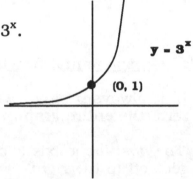

If b is any number greater than 1, $f(x) = b^x$ is an exponential function whose graph looks similar to the illustration above. From the graph, we can discover some important properties.

Properties of the function $f(x) = b^x$, when b is greater than 1:

1. b^x is <u>always positive</u>, whether the value of x is positive, negative or zero (the entire graph is above the x-axis).

2. As x gets bigger in a positive direction, b^x gets bigger even faster (the graph swoops up sharply as we go to the right). For example, $3^{10} = 59,049$.

3. As x gets bigger in the *negative* direction, b^x gets very close to 0. In other words, the x-axis is a horizontal asymptote. For example, 3^{-10} is approximately 0.0000169, or more precisely:
$$3^{-10} = \frac{1}{3^{10}} = \frac{1}{59,049}$$
Note, however, that the horizontal asymptote is approached as the graph goes off to the left, but not as it goes off to the right—as it would in the graph of a rational function such as those we studied in Chapter 5.

4. If $a < c$, then $b^a < b^c$. In other words, as x increases, b^x also increases (the graph goes continuously uphill from left to right).

5. $f(0) = 1$ (the y-intercept of the graph is (0, 1)) for any value of b.

If b is a *positive* number *less than 1*, we also have an exponential function $f(x) = b^x$, but it looks like a mirror image of what we get when b > 1. Here is the graph of $f(x) = 0.5^x$.

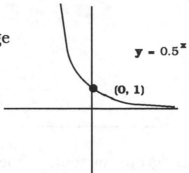

$y = 0.5^x$

(0, 1)

Properties of exponential functions $f(x) = b^x$ when b is between 0 and 1.

1. b^x is <u>always positive</u>, whether the value of x is positive, negative, or zero (the entire graph is above the x-axis).

2. The *positive* x-axis is a horizontal asymptote, this time as the graph goes off to the right. For example, 0.5^{10} is approximately 0.0009766, or very close to 0.

3. As x gets bigger in a negative direction, b^x gets bigger even faster (the graph swoops up sharply as we move to the left). For example, $0.5^{-10} = 1024$.

4. If a < c, then $b^c < b^a$. In other words, as x increases, b^x *decreases* (the graph goes *downhill* from left to right).

5. $f(0) = 1$ (the y-intercept of the graph is (0, 1)) for any value of b.

For any exponential function $f(x) = b^x$, the number b is called the *base* of the exponential function. We cannot use a negative number as a base, because we already know (for example) that we cannot raise -2 to the $\frac{1}{2}$ power. Theoretically, we could use 1 as our base, but that would lead to a very boring function (1^x is always equal to 1, no matter what x is). So we have just two flavors of exponential functions: the kind with the base greater than 1, and the kind with the base between 0 and 1.

Exponential and Logarithmic Functions, Exercise 1. Exponential Functions.

1. Place the correct sign (< or >) between the two numbers.

    a. 5^{-2} 5^{-3}

    b. 5^{-2} 5^3

    c. $\left(\frac{1}{5}\right)^2$ $\left(\frac{1}{5}\right)^3$

    d. $\left(\frac{1}{5}\right)^{-2}$ $\left(\frac{1}{5}\right)^{-3}$

    e. $\left(\frac{1}{5}\right)^{-2}$ $\left(\frac{1}{5}\right)^3$

2. Solve the equations.

    a. $\left(\frac{2}{3}\right)^x = 1$

    b. $\left(\frac{2}{3}\right)^{x-5} = 1$

    c. $\left(\frac{2}{3}\right)^{x-5} = 0$

    d. $\left(\frac{2}{3}\right)^{x-5} = -\frac{2}{3}$

Exponential Equations

An exponential equation is an equation where the unknown is all or part of an exponent. The most important rule for solving exponential equations is:

$$\text{If } 0 < b \neq 1, \text{ and } b^a = b^c,$$

$$\text{then } a = c.$$

•Example:

Solve:
1. $3^x = 3^6$
2. $4^{x-2} = 4^{4-x}$
3. $2^{2x+1} = \frac{1}{2}$
4. $2^{3x-1} = 4^{x+1}$
5. $8^{x+2} = 4^{2x+3}$

SOLUTION:

1. By the rule above, $x = 6$.
2. By the rule above, $x - 2 = 4 - x$. Therefore:

$$2x = 6$$

$$x = 3.$$

3. Before we can use our rule, both sides of the equation must have the same base. We can accomplish that goal by changing the to $\frac{1}{2}$ to 2^{-1}.

So:
$$2^{2x+1} = 2^{-1}$$
$$2x + 1 = -1$$
$$2x = -2$$
$$x = -1.$$

4. Both sides can have the same base by changing the 4 on the right to 2^2. So:

$$2^{3x-1} = (2^2)^{x+1}$$

$$2^{3x-1} = 2^{2x+2}$$

$$3x - 1 = 2x + 2$$

$$x = 3.$$

5. This time to have both sides with the same base, we express both sides as a power of 2:

$$8^{x+2} = 4^{2x+3}$$

$$(2^3)^{x+2} = (2^2)^{2x+3}$$

$$3x + 6 = 4x + 6$$

$$x = 0$$

Exponential and Logarithmic Functions, Exercise 2. Exponential Equations.

Solve.

1. $4^{x-1} = 4^3$ 2. $4^{x-1} = 4^{2x-6}$

3. $9^{x^2} = 3^x$ 4. $(\frac{1}{3})^{2x} = -9$

5. $2^{x+3} - 5 = 3$ 6. $5^{2x} - 24 = 2 - 5^2$

7. $9^x = (\frac{1}{27})^{x+5}$ 8. $2^{x+11} + 10 = -2^1$

9. $2^{2x-5} = 32^{x-3}$ 10. $4^{2x-5} = 32^{x-3}$

Part 3   **Logarithms**

Suppose a and b are two positive numbers, with b not equal to 1. Then the logarithm (or log), base b, of a is the power to which we must raise b in order to get a. The phrase "logarithm, base b" is usually abbreviated by the notation log_b, with the "b" used as a subscript below and to the right of the word "log". Also, we often put the number "a", after the "log_b", in parentheses for the sake of clarity. HOWEVER:

BIG TIME WARNING

$log_b(27)$ does NOT mean log *times* 27! The parentheses in this case have nothing to do with multiplication! "$log_b(27)$" is read as "log_b OF 27".

•Examples:

$2^3 = 8$, so $log_2 8 = 3$.

$17^0 = 1$, so $log_{17} 1 = 0$.

$0.7^4 = 0.2401$, so $log_{0.7}(0.2401) = 4$.

$0.8^{-3} = 1.953125$, so $log_{0.8} 1.953125 = -3$.

$22^{0.9165883} = 17$, so $log_{22} 17 = 0.9165883$.

$86^{-0.6725412} = 0.05$, so $log_{86} 0.05 = -0.6725412$.

The examples above lead us to the **Fundamental Equivalence** between logarithms and exponents:

$$b^a = c$$
means exactly the same as
$$log_b c = a$$

if b is any positive number except 1, and if a is any positive number at all, then $\log_b a$ exists. In other words, given any positive numbers a and b , with b not equal to 1, you can find some power of b which is equal to a. That power (the exponent) is $\log_b a$.

If we choose some positive value for b and hold it constant, then we can think of $\log_b x$ as a function:

$f(x) = \log_b x$ = the power of b which equals x.

Here are graphs of the function $f(x) = \log_3 x$

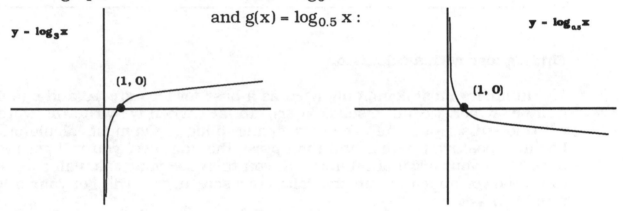

and $g(x) = \log_{0.5} x$:

These graphs illustrate several important properties of the function $f(x) = \log_b x$:

1. The domain of $\log_b x$ is all *positive* numbers (zero is not in the domain because you can't raise a non-zero number to a power and get zero.)
2. $\log_b 1$ is always 0 no matter what b is (because $b^0 = 1$).
3. No two different numbers have the same $\log_b$. In other words, if $\log_b x = \log_b y$, then x = y.
4. If b is greater than 1:
   (a.) If x is less than 1, then $\log_b x$ is negative. If x is greater than 1, log x is positive.
   (b.) As x gets very small, $\log_b x$ becomes a large negative number (the graph squeezes against the y-axis on the way down).
   (c.) If a < c, then $\log_b a < \log_b c$ -in other words, as x increases, $\log_b x$ also increases (the graph is uphill from left-to-right all the way).
   (d.) As x gets very large, the value of $\log_b x$ increases, but the rate of increase gets slower and slower (the graph flattens out to the right).
5. If b is less than 1:
   (a.) If x less than 1, then $\log_b x$ is positive. If x is greater than 1, $\log_b x$ is negative.
   (b.) As x gets very small, $\log_b x$ becomes large (the graph squeezes against the y-axis on the way up).
   (c.) As x increases, the $\log_b x$ decreases (the graph is downhill from left to right all the way).
   (d.) As x gets very large, the value of $\log_b x$ decreases, but the rate of decrease gets slower and slower (the graph flattens out to the right).

Finding logs with a calculator.

The numbers most commonly used as a base for logs are 10 and e (a strange number which we will discuss later). In fact, when we write the word *log* with no subscript at all, we are referring to $\log_{10}$. On most calculators, if you key in a positive number and then press the "log" key, you will get the log base 10 of your original number. (If you then use your calculator to raise 10 to the power appearing on the calculator screen, you will get your original number.)

•Examples:

log of 10 is 1,	and $10^1 = 10.$
log 1 is 0,	and $10^0 = 1.$
log of 0.1 is -1,	and $10^{-1} = 0.1.$
log of 139,402 is 5.144269,	and $10^{5.144269} = 139,402$

(The last equation is approximate, but it is accurate out to 8 decimal points.)

Finding logs to other bases.

We can find other bases by using the:

Change of Base Formula

$$\log_b a = \frac{\log a}{\log b} \quad \left(\text{Recall } \frac{\log a}{\log b} = \frac{\log_{10} a}{\log_{10} b}\right)$$

In other words, we can get log base **b** of **a** by first finding the log (base 10) of a, then dividing by the log of the new base.

•Examples:

Find the following logs, and check the answer by using the
Fundamental Equivalence:

1. $\log_7 23$

2. $\log_{23} 7$

3. $\log_5(0.11)$

4. $\log_{0.11} 5$

SOLUTION

1. Log 23 = 1.3617278, and log 7 = 0.845098. Therefore
   $\log_7 23 = \frac{1.3617278}{0.845098} = 1.6113253$. Checking, we find that
   $7^{1.6113253} = 23$, as it should.

2. Using the same numbers as in #1, we get $\log_{23} 7 = 0.6206071$, and
   we find that $23^{0.6206071} = 7$.

3. Log 0.11 = -0.9586073, and log 5 = 0.69897. Therefore,
   $\log_5 (0.11) = -1.371457$, and $5^{-1.371457} = 0.11$.

4. Using the same values as in #3, we get $\log_{0.11} (5) = -0.7291515$,
   and $0.11^{-0.7291515} = 5$.

Exponential and Logarithmic Functions, Exercise 3.

Write the equivalent
exponential equation:

1. $\log_3 x = y$
2. $\log_x y = 3$
3. $\log_y (x - 2) = 3$
4. $\log_5 y = x - 2$
5. $\log_{(x-1)}(y + 4) = 6$

Write the equivalent
logarithmic equation:

6. $4^x = y$
7. $y^4 = x$
8. $(y - 1)^4 = x$
9. $x^{y+2} = 7$
10. $5^{x-3} = 2y - 4$

Use a calculator to find:

11. log 15
12. $\log_{15} (12)$
13. $\log_{0.7} (86)$
14. $\log_6 (0.01)$
15. $\log_6 (18)$

Without a calculator, find:

16. $\log_{\sqrt{2}} (1)$.
17. $\log_{\sqrt{2}} (-1)$.
18. If $\log_3 x = \log_3 7$, what can we say of x?
19. Which is greater, $\log_8 (7)$ or $\log_8 (8)$?
20. Which is greater, $\log_{0.8} (7)$ or $\log_{0.8} (8)$?

We can use the same transformation rules which we discussed back in Chapter 5 to get graphs of different variations of exponential and logarithmic functions.

•Examples:

Graph the following functions:
a. $f(x) = 2^{x-3}$

b. $f(x) = 2^x - 3$

c. $g(x) = 3\log_{10}(2 - x)$

SOLUTIONS:

a. According to our transformation rules, this graph is a graph of $y = 2^x$, shifted to the right by three units. Notice that the negative x-axis is still a horizontal asymptote; the graph simply slides to the right along the same asymptote.

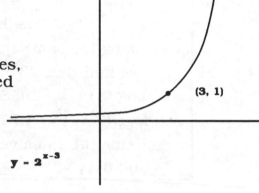

b. The rules say that we take the graph of $y = 2$, and shift it downward by 3 units. The shift will cause the line $y = -3$ to become the new horizontal asymptote to the left.

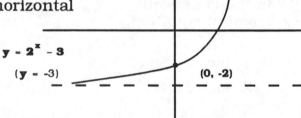

c. We begin with $y = \log_{10} x$. Then we must successively:
(1.) Add 2 to x, which shifts left by 2.
(2.) Change x to -x, which means reflect in the y-axis (left and right).
(3.) Multiply the function by 3, which means stretch the graph vertically by a factor of 3.

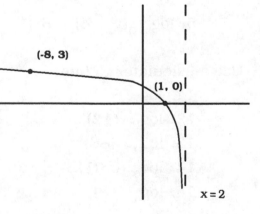

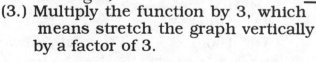

132

Exponential and Logarithmic Functions, Exercise 4. Graphs of Exponential &
Logarithmic Functions.

Sketch the graphs of the following:

1. $f(x) = 4^{x+2}$

2. $f(x) = 0.8^x + 3$

3. $f(x) = \log_5(-x)$

4. $g(x) = 4\log_{0.3}x$

5. $f(x) = \frac{2}{3}(5^x)$

6. $f(x) = -0.75^x$

7. $g(x) = \log_{10}x - 2$

8. $h(x) = \log_{0.6}(x - 3)$

9. $f(x) = 3^{x+1} - 2$

10. $f(x) = \log_4(-x) + 1$

11. $f(x) = -5(0.6^{x-2})$

12. $f(x) = \frac{1}{4}\log_{0.3}(3 - x)$

Part 5	**Properties of Logarithms**

Just because of the way logarithms are defined and derived, they possess
some interesting properties. The most important of these properties are
listed below. For any numbers a, b, c, and p such that the given expressions
are defined, we have the following identities:

1. $\log_b b^a = a$

2. $b^{\log_b a} = a$

3. $\log_b(ac) = \log_b a + \log_b c$

4. $\log_b(\frac{a}{c}) = \log_b a - \log_b c$

5. $\log_b(a^p) = (p)\log_b a$

BIG TIME WARNING

We also have a couple of important NON-indentities: $\log_b(a + c)$ and
$\log_b(a - c)$ cannot be simplified <u>in any way</u> in terms of the separate
logs of a and c!

Properties 1 and 2 above follow directly from the Fundamental Equivalence
given in the Part 3 of this Chapter. The equivalent equation for Property 1
is $b^a = b^a$, which is obviously true. The equivalent equation for Property 2 is
$\log_b a = \log_b a$, which is equally obvious.

The derivations of the other properties are slightly more complicated; we
show how the get Property 3 as an example:

By Property 2, we can express ac as $(b^{\log_b a})(b^{\log_b c})$. Therefore,

$$\log_b ac = \log_b\left[\left(b^{\log_b a}\right)\left(b^{\log_b c}\right)\right]$$

$$= \log_b\left[b^{\log_b a + \log_b c}\right] \quad \text{(Rule of Exponents)}$$

$$= \log_b a + \log_b c \quad \text{(Property 1)}$$

We can use these properties to solve several kinds of interesting problems:

•Example:

Simplify the following expression into one logarithm:

$$2\log_b 5 - \log_b 16.$$

SOLUTION:

By Property 5, $2\log_b 5 = \log_b 5^2 = \log_b 25$. By Property 4,
$\log_b 25 - \log_b 16 = \log_b \frac{25}{16}$. Therefore, $2\log_b 5 - \log_b 16 = \log_b \frac{25}{16}$.

•Example:

Suppose, without knowing the value of b, we know that:

$$\log_b 2 = 0.3526$$
$$\log_b 3 = 0.5588$$
$$\log_b 25 = 1.6373$$

Then find the following :

    a. $\log_b 6$

    b. $\log_b 9$

    c. $\log_b 0.8$

SOLUTION:

a. Since $6 = 2 \cdot 3$, Property 3 tells us that
$$\log_b 6 = \log_b(2 \cdot 3)$$
$$= \log_b 2 + \log_b 3$$
$$= 0.3526 + 0.5588$$
$$= 0.9114$$

b. Since $9 = 3^2$, we can reason as follows :
$$\log_b 9 = \log_b(3)^2$$
$$= 2\log_b 3$$
$$= 1.1176.$$

134

c. If we knew $\log_b 4$ and $\log_b 5$, we could use Property 4 to express $\log 0.8$ as $\log_b(\frac{4}{5}) = \log_b 4 - \log 5$. We can get $\log_b 5$, because $5 = 25^{\frac{1}{2}}$, and so $\log_b 5 = \frac{1}{2}\log 25 = \frac{1}{2}(1.6373) = 0.81865$. Similarly, $\log_b 4 = \log_b 2^2 = 2\log_b 2 = 2(0.3526) = 0.7052$. Putting it together :

$$\log_b 0.8 = \log_b(\tfrac{4}{5})$$
$$= \log_b 4 - \log_b 5$$
$$= -0.11345$$

Exponential and Logarithmic Functions, Exercise 5. Properties of Logarithms.

In 1 - 4, express each in terms of separate logs of x, y, and z if possible.

1. $\log_b(\frac{x^2}{\sqrt{y}})$

2. $\log_b(xy^2z^3)$

3. $\log_b(x^2 - \sqrt{y})$

4. $\log_b(x^b)$

In 5 - 8, express each as a single log.

5. $3\log_b x - 2\log_b y + \frac{1}{2}\log_b z$

6. $(x)\log_b y$

7. $\frac{1}{2}\log_b y^2 - 3\log_b x$

8. $(\log_b x)(\log_b b^5)$

In 9 - 12, use the following values.

$$\log_b 2 = 0.5489$$
$$\log_b \sqrt{3} = 0.4350$$
$$\log_b 49 = 3.0817$$

Then find :

9. $\log_b 1.5$ 10. $\log_b \sqrt{7}$

11. $\log_b 42$ 12. $\log_b(\frac{18}{7})$

The Fundamental Equivalence between logarithmic and exponential equations, along with the properties of logarithms which were discussed in Part 5, give us powerful tools to solve equations in which the unknown is part of an exponent or part of a log.

Example:

Solve: $2^{x-1} = 5$.

SOLUTION:

The equivalent logarithmic equation is $\log_2 5 = x - 1$. By using a calculator along with the Base Changing formula given in the Part 3 of this Chapter, we can get the value of $\log_2 5$:

$$\log_2 5 = \frac{\log 5}{\log 2} = \frac{.69897}{.30103} \cong 2.3219$$

Therefore we have $x - 1 = 2.3219$
and $x = 3.3219$.

• Example:

Solve: $3 \cdot 5^{2x-1} = 93$.

SOLUTION:

We cannot use the Fundamental Equivalence immediately, because the original equation is not in the proper form for us to do so. We have to get rid of the "3" on the left-hand side first. So we divide both sides by 3, to get:

$$5^{2x-1} = 31$$

The fundamental equivalence then gives us:

$2x - 1 = \log_5 31 = 2.13366$ (calculator and Base Change formula)
$2x = 3.13366$
$x = 1.56683$

•Examples:

> Solve: a. $\log_3 x = 2$
>   b. $\log_x 16 = 2$.
>
> SOLUTIONS:
>
> a. The equivalent equation is $x = 3^2$, or $x = 9$.
> b. The equivalent equation is $x^2 = 16$. The solutions to this equation
> are 4 and -4, but <u>-4 is not a legal solution to the original equation</u>,
> because x was the base of the log function, and the base of a log
> function can never be negative. Therefore, x = 4 is the only
> solution.

•Example

> Solve: $\log_2 x + \log_2(x + 3) = 2$.
>
> SOLUTION:
>
> Before we can use the Fundamental Equivalence, we have to get just a
> single log on the left-hand side of the equation. From the properties
> discussed in Part 5, we can convert the equation to:
>
> $$\log_2(x^2 + 3x) = 2$$
>
> The Fundamental Equivalence now gives:
>
> $$x^2 + 3x = 2^2,$$
> $$\text{or}$$
> $$x^2 + 3x - 4 = 0.$$
>
> The expression on the left-hand side of the equation factors into
> $(x + 4)(x - 1)$, so the solutions are -4 and 1. However, the original
> equation has $\log_2 x$ in it, we can't take the log of a negative number.
> Therefore, x = -4 is not a legal solution. The only solution to the
> original equation is x = 1.

> **BIG TIME WARNING**
>
> Answers which cause the original equation to have the log of a negative
> number are illegal. But that doesn't mean that the unknown itself has
> to be positive. For example, x = -2 is a perfectly acceptable solution to
> the equation $\log_5(x + 3) = 0$. On the other hand, x = 1 is not a legal
> solution to $2\log_4(x - 3) = 5$, even though 1 is a positive number,
> because if x = 1, then x - 3 = -2.

Exponential and Logarithmic Functions, Exercise 6. Solving Logarithmic and Exponential Equations.

Solve:

1. $10^{2x} = 1000$

2. $10^{2x} = 55$

3. $10^{2x} + 3 = 55$

4. $5^{2x-1} = 55$

5. $5^{2x-1} = \frac{1}{55}$

6. $6(5^{2x-1}) = 33$

7. $\log_3 x = 4$

8. $\log_x 81 = 4$

9. $\log_5(x + 1) - \log_5(25 - x) = 2$

10. $2\log_5(x + 1) - \log_5 x = 1$

11. $\log_{18}(x + 1) + \log_{18}(x - 2) = 1$

12. $\frac{\log_7(x+1)}{2} = 1$

Part 7   **Applications of Logarithmic and Exponential Functions**

There are many applications for logarithmic and exponential functions in the physical, biological, and social sciences. These applications almost always use a logarithm base called "e", which is an ugly-looking number equal to approximately 2.7182818 (like π, e actually runs on forever). The reasons for using such a strange looking number as the base of a logarithm have to do primarily with calculus, so it is best just to accept it for now! You can get logs to the base e, called *natural logarithms*, on most calculators by keying in the number whose log you want, and then pressing the "ln" key. In what follows, we shall frequently use the notation "ln" as an abbreviation for "$\log_e$".

In this chapter, we will deal with only two of the many applications which use logarithmic and exponential equations. Both topics may be grouped under the heading of "exponential growth and decay". Suppose a quantity grows or declines in proportion to the size of the quantity. In that case, we say that the quantity is growing or decreasing exponentially. Over any given period of time, we want an equation that describes the change in the quantity. The correct equation is set up this way. Let:

Q_0 = the quantity at the beginning of the time period.
Q = the quantity at the end of the time period.
t = the length of the time in the time period.

Then the two Q's are related by the equation

$$Q = Q_0\, e^{kt}$$

if the quantity is increasing, and

$$Q = Q_0\, e^{-kt}$$

if the quantity is decreasing. The letter "k" stands for a constant which must be determined by knowing something about the rate of growth or decrease.

138

•Example

> The population of a certain city is growing at a constant exponential rate. Suppose the population was 10,000 on January 1, 1985, and had grown to 11,000 by January 1, 1990.
>
> a. What can we expect the population to be on January 1, 1997?
>
> b. When can we expect the population to reach 15,000?
>
> SOLUTION
>
> a. Our knowledge of the population on January 1, 1985, and on January 1, 1990, enables us to set up the growth equation with the following values:
> $$Q_0 = 10,000$$
> $$Q = 11,000$$
> $$t = 5 \text{ (1985 to 1990, measured in years)}$$
> We therefore get the equation $11,000 = 10,000e^{k(5)}$, where the only unknown is k. We can solve for k using the approach learned in Part 6:
>
> $$11,000 = 10,000e^{k(5)}$$
> $$1.1 = e^{k(5)} \qquad \text{(divide by 10,000)}$$
> $$\ln(1.1) = 5k \qquad \text{(Fundamental Equivalence)}$$
> $$.09531 = 5k \qquad \text{(calculator)}$$
> $$k = .019062$$
> Now that we have a value for k, we set up the equation again to show the growth from 1990 to 1997. In this case:
> $$Q_0 = 11,000$$
> $$Q = \text{the unknown}$$
> $$t = 7$$
> $$k = 0.019062 \text{ (calculated in the previous step)}$$
> Now we just plug all the numbers into the calculator and get the answer:
> $$Q = 11,000e^{(0.019062)(7)}$$
> $$= 11,000 \ (1.1427461)$$
> $$= 12,570$$
>
> b. In this case the unknown is t, because we are asked when something is going to happen. So we need values for the other three variables in the formula—namely Q, Q_0, and k. We already calculated k in Part a, and Q and Q_0 are given in the problem. We have:
> $$Q = 15,000$$
> $$Q_0 = 11,000$$
> $$k = 0.019062$$
>
> So our equation is:
> $$15,000 = 11,000e^{0.019062t}$$

To solve this for t, we put the equation in the form needed to use the Fundamental Equivalence. So we divide both sides by 11,000 to get:

$$1.36364 = e^{0.019062t}$$

Now we use the Fundamental Equivalence and solve for t:

$$\ln 1.36364 = 0.019062t$$
$$0.019062t = 0.3101549$$
$$t = 16.27$$

So t = 16.27, which means the population will reach 15,000 sometime in the year 1990 + 16.27 years, or the year 2006. (Just for fun, try to verify that the exact date will be April 9, 2006!)

•Example:

Suppose a radioactive substance is decaying at a rate such that it takes 750 years to decay down to half the original quantity (this means that the <u>half-life</u> is 750 years). If we start with 24 grams of the substance, how much will be left after 300 years?

Once again, the value of k is not directly known, but it can be calculated from the information given. When the problem tells us that it takes 750 years for the substance to decay to half of its original quantity, it doesn't say what the original quantity is. But we can choose any number we want, and we will get the same value of k no matter what we choose as Q_0. It turns out the easiest thing to do is to let $Q_0 = 1$, so that $Q = 0.5$ after 750 years. Setting it up:

$$Q = 0.5$$
$$Q_0 = 1$$
$$t = 750$$

So our equation is $0.5 = 1e^{-k(750)}$, which then translates to

$$\ln(0.5) = -750k$$
$$-0.69315 = -750k$$
$$k = 0.000924196.$$

Now we set the equation up again, this time using t = 300, k = 0.000924, and $Q_0 = 24$. This gives:

$$Q = 24e^{-(0.000924196)(300)}$$
$$= 24(0.75786)$$
$$= 18.19 \text{ grams}$$

Exponential and Logarithmic Functions, Exercise 7. Applications of Logarithmic and Exponential Functions.

In all exercises, assume that the quantity discussed is changing at an exponential rate.

1. A bacteria colony has 10,000 bacteria at noon, and 13,000 at 2:00 P.M. How many bacteria will be in the colony be at 4:00 P.M.? HINTS: You can do this without logarithms at all, and the answer is NOT 16,000.

2. The population doubles every 23 years. How long does it take the population to triple?

3. In 1900, the population of Los Angeles was 102,479. By 1950, the population was 1,970,358. If the population had continued to increase at the same rate as it did between 1900 and 1950, how many people would be living in Los Angeles in 1993?

4. Using the information from question #3, in what year did the population of Los Angeles reach 500,000?

5. The half-life of a particular radioactive substance is 22 days. If you have a 12-gram sample of the substance, how much will be left undecayed after 2 weeks (14 days)?

6. Using the information from question #5, how long would it take the 12-gram sample to decay down to 1 gram?

7. Again using the information from question #5, how long ago was the 12-gram sample as big as 20 grams?

8. Assume that the IQ of a writer of a math textbook decreases exponentially according to the amount of time he/she has spent working on a book. Suppose the writer's IQ was 115 when work began, and 111 one month afterwards. What is the writer's IQ now that the book is finished (six months after it was begun)?

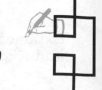

Final Assessment Test

1. Circle each number below which belongs in the interval $(-\infty, 3)$:

    a. -2   b. 3   c. 1.654321   d. -999.3

    e. 0   f. 8   g. 2.99999

2. Solve: $|3x + 2| = 22$

3. Express $\dfrac{1}{\sqrt[5]{x^8}}$ as x with an exponent.

4. Define, with functional notation, the function which adds 4 to the input number (x) and then takes the square root of the result.

5. If $f(x) = x^2 - 3$, and $g(x) = x + 1$, then find:

    a. $(f + g)(x)$
    b. $(f - g)(x)$
    c. $(fg)(x)$
    d. $\dfrac{f}{g}(x)$
    e. $f(g(x))$
    f. $g(f(x))$
    g. $f(x - 2)$
    h. $g(f(-4))$

6. Find the domain of $h(x) = \log\left(\dfrac{x+3}{x^2}\right)$.

7. Given the graph:

    a. Approximate f(1).
    b. State all points of discontinuity.
    c. Solve the inequality f(x)>0.

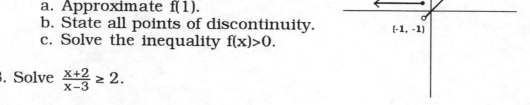

8. Solve $\dfrac{x+2}{x-3} \geq 2$.

9. Do the following divisions, giving both the quotient and the remainder:

    a. $(3x^5 - x^3 + x^2 + x - 9) \div (x^2 - 2)$
    b. $(3x^5 - x^3 + x^2 + x - 9) \div (x + 2)$

10. a. Factor the polynomial $x^4 - 4x^3 + 4x^2 + 36x - 117$ completely
    (some of the factors may contain complex numbers).
    b. Graph the polynomial from Part a.

11. Graph $\frac{2x^2-18}{x^2-1}$.

12. Find all six trigonometric functions of an angle whose terminal side contains
    the point (4, -7).

13. Graph $y = \cos(x - 2\pi)$.

14. Simplify $\tan^2 y(\frac{1}{\cos^2 y} + \frac{1}{\sin^2 y})$.

15. If A is in QI, B is in QIV, tan A = 2, and sin B = -0.4, find tan (A + B).

16. Draw the graph for $y = 3^{x+1} - 1$.

17. a. Give the equivalent exponential form for $\log_x 4 = y$.
    b. Give the equivalent logarithmic form of $13^{x-1} = k$.

18. a. Solve $\log_8(x - 1) + \log_8(x + 1) = 1$.
    b. Solve $2e^{5x} = 0.73576$.

Answers

Preliminary Ideas, Exercise 1. Page 3.

1. a. [-3, -1] **b.** (-3, -1]
 c. (-3, -1) **d.** [-3, ∞)
 e. [-2, 0) **f.** (-∞, -2)

2. a. (-∞, 4) **b.** [0, ∞)
 c. (0, 5] **d.** [-2, 1)
 e. (0, 1) **f.** [-2, 5]

3.

a.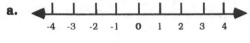

b.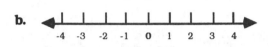

c.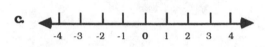

d.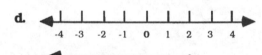

e.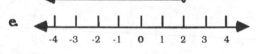

f.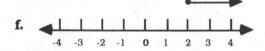

4. a. $-5 < x < -3$ **b.** $-2 \le x \le 6$
 c. $0 < x < 3$ **d.** $-5 \le x < 0$
 e. $x \le 0$ **f.** $x > 5$

Preliminary Ideas, Exercise 2. Page 8.

1. a. x if $x \ge 0$ **b.** x if x<0
  -x if $x < 0$ -x if x≥0
 c. 10 - x if $x \le 10$ **d.** 3x + 10 if $x \ge -\frac{10}{3}$
  x - 10 if $x > 10$ -3x - 10 if $x < -\frac{10}{3}$
 e. -6 - 2x if $x \le -3$
  2x + 6 if $x > -3$

2. a. 2 **b.** 2
 c. 1 **d.** 0
 e. 20 **f.** 1

3. a. 4, -4 **b.** 0, 10
 c. 0, 5 **d.** no solution
 e. 6, $\frac{4}{3}$ **f.** -1
 g. no solution **h.** 0, 6

Preliminary Ideas, Exercise 3. Page 11.

1. 3 **2.** undefined
3. -3 **4.** 2

5. -2 **6.** -2
7. 5 **8.** 8
9. undefined **10.** 4
11. -4 **12.** 3
13. -3 **14.** 0
15. 32 **16.** 64
17. $\frac{1}{9}$ **18.** -32
19. undefined **20.** 8

Preliminary Ideas, Exercise 4. Page 15 .

1. rational, real, complex
2. integer, rational, real, complex
3. complex
4. integer, rational, real, complex
5. complex
6. integer, rational, real, complex
7. complex
8. real, complex
9. integer, rational, real, complex
10. integer, rational, real, complex
11. rational, real, complex
12. complex
13. real, complex
14. complex
15. real, complex
16. 3 **17.** $3i$
18. $2 + i$ **19.** $\frac{2}{3} - i$
20. $4 - 5\sqrt{6}\, i$ **21.** $3 + \sqrt{7}$
22. $3 + \sqrt{7}\, i$ **23.** $\frac{2+\sqrt{12}}{5}$
24. $\frac{2}{5} + \frac{2\sqrt{3}}{5} i$ **25.** $6\sqrt{2}\, i$
26. $-29 - 22i$ **27.** $-4 - \frac{16}{5} i$
28. $60 - 35i$ **29.** $6 + 4i$
30. $\frac{-1869}{260} - \frac{63}{260} i$ **31.** $4 - \frac{21}{5} i$
32. $\frac{13}{25} - \frac{34}{25} i$ **33.** $\frac{38}{21} + \frac{58}{7} i$
34. $-2 + 10i$ **35.** $4 - \frac{29}{5} i$
36. $\frac{17}{3} - \frac{48}{7} i$ **37.** $-\frac{25}{4} - 5i$
38. $\frac{60}{193} + \frac{35}{193} i$ **39.** $\frac{13}{3} - \frac{36}{7} i$

Functions, Exercise 1. Page 18.

1. a. 2 **b.** 5
 c. -25 **d.** 0
 e. 17 **f.** 10

2. a. 6 **b.** -4
 c. $-\frac{3}{2}$ **d.** -1

3. a. 8 **b.** 13
 c. 7 **d.** $\frac{65}{9}$

4. a. f(x)=x+3 **b.** f(x)=(x+3)² or
   x² + 6x + 9
 c. $f(x) = \frac{x+3}{12-x}$ **d.** f(x)=x⁵-4x+6
 e. f(x)= -45 **f.** f(x)= x

Functions, Excerise 2. Page 21.
1. **a.** $2x$ **b.** 2
 c. x^2-1 **d.** $\frac{x+1}{x-1}$
 e. $x-2$ **f.** $-2x+2$
 g. $4x-1$ **h.** 1
 i. 2
2. **a.** $32x$ **b.** $28x$
 c. $60x^2$ **d.** 15
 e. $30x-3$ **f.** $-4x$
 g. $5x$ **h.** $\frac{x+1}{30x}$
 i. 32
3. **a.** $x+3$ **b.** $3-x$
 c. $3x$ **d.** $\frac{3}{x}$
 e. 0 **f.** $-2x$
 g. $4x$ **h.** $\frac{x+1}{3}$
 i. 4
4. **a.** $3x^2+3x-19$ **b.** $-3x^2+x+19$
 c. $6x^3+2x^2-38x$ **d.** $\frac{2x}{3x^2+x-19}$
 e. $2x-3$ **f.** $-6x^2-2x+38$
 g. $3x^2+4x-19$ **h.** $\frac{x+1}{2x}$
 i. -13
5. **a.** $\frac{6x-17}{18x^5+3x^2-19x}$ **b,** $\frac{1}{18x^5+3x^2-19x}$
 d. $\frac{3x-8}{3x-9}$ **f.** $\frac{-6x+18}{18x^5+3x^2-19x}$
 i. $-\frac{11}{2}$

Functions, Exercise 3. Page 23.
1. **a.** $x-6$ **b.** $x-6$
 c. $\frac{2x-9}{3}$ or $\frac{2x}{3}-3$
 d. $-3x+9$
2. **a.** $4x^2+12x+5$ **b.** $4x^2+8x+1$
 c. $2x^2+8x+1$ **d.** x^2+8x
3. **a.** $\frac{x^2-4x+5}{x-4}$ **b.** $\frac{x^2-2x+5}{x-2}$
 c. 10
4. **a.** $83,299$ **b.** $83,299$
 c. $83,299$ **d.** -1
5. **a.** 69 **b.** 49
 c. $\frac{3x^2}{x-4}+\frac{3y^2}{y-4}$
 d. $\frac{3(x+y)^2}{x+y-4}$ or $\frac{3x^2+6xy+3y^2}{x+y-4}$
 e. $\frac{3(x-2)^2}{x-6}$ or $\frac{3x^2-12x+12}{x-6}$
 f. $\frac{3x^2+6x-24}{x-4}$ or $\frac{3x^2}{x-4}+6$
 g. $\frac{3x^2-2x+8}{x-4}$ or $\frac{3x^2}{x-4}-2$

Functions, Exercise 4. Page 28.
1. **a.** $16-x$ **b.** $-x$
 c. $-x^2+64$ **d.** 14
2. **a.** $x+3$ **b.** $x+3$
 c. x^2+3x+2 **d.** 5

3. **a.** $4x^2+4$ **b.** $2x^2+8$
 c. $2x^3+8x$ **d.** 20
4. **a.** x^{-36} **b.** x^{-36}
 c. x^9
5. **a.** $(2x-17)^{12}$ **b.** $2x^{12}-17$
 c. $2x^{13}-17x^{12}$
6. **a.** $\frac{3}{x^2+2x-3}$ **b.** $\frac{9}{x^2}+\frac{6}{x}-3$
 c. $3x+6-\frac{9}{x}$ **d.** $\frac{3}{5}$

7. **a.** $\frac{x}{x-2}$ **b.** $\frac{x+1}{x-1}-1$ or $\frac{2}{x-1}$
 c. $x+1$ **d.** undefined!
8. **a.** x **b.** x
 c. $\frac{3x^2-10x-25}{3}$ **d.** 2

Functions, Exercise 5. Page 31.
1. All real numbers except 1, or $(-\infty, 1)\cup(1, \infty)$.
2. All real numbers except -5, or $(-\infty, -5)\cup(-5, \infty)$.
3. $[3, \infty)$ 4. $(3, \infty)$
5. $(3, \infty)$ 6. $(-\infty, \infty)$ (all real numbers)
7. $(-\infty, 0)\cup(0, \infty)$ 8. $(-\infty, \infty)$
9. $[3, \infty)$ 10. $(-\infty, 4]$

Functions, Exercise 6. Page 34.
1. $x \longleftrightarrow x$
   $2x \longleftrightarrow \frac{1}{2}x$
   $x+12 \longleftrightarrow x-12$
   $2x-7 \longleftrightarrow \frac{1}{2}(x+7)$
   $\frac{x-3}{x+2} \longleftrightarrow \frac{-2x-3}{x-1}$
   $\frac{3x+2}{x-1} \longleftrightarrow \frac{x+2}{x-3}$
2. **a.** 0 **b.** 6
 c. 1

Functions, Exercise 7. Page 38.
1. **a.** iii   **b.** iv
 c. i   **d.** ii
2. **a.** -3 **b.** -1
 c. undefined   **d.** 0
3. a, b, and d are functions.

Functions, Exercise 8. Page 41.
1. $(-\infty, 1]$ and $(2, \infty)$ 2. $[-1, 1]$ and $[2, \infty)$
3. $(-\infty, 2)$ and $[2, \infty)$ 4. $(-\infty, 2)$ and $(2, \infty)$
5. $(-\infty, \infty)$; no discontinuities
6. $(-\infty, \infty)$; no discontinuities
7. $(-\infty, -1)$ and $(-1, \infty)$; discontinuity at -1
8. $(-\infty, -1)$ and $(-1, \infty)$; discontinuity at -1
9. $(-\infty, -1)$, $(-1, 1)$, and $(1, \infty)$; discontinuities at -1 and 1.

Functions, Exercise 9. Page 43.

1. -7
2. 1
3. 16
4. 8.9
5. 10
6. 2
7. 4
8. 16
9. 10
10. 12

11. $f(x) = \begin{cases} -x & x < 0 \\ x & x \geq 0 \end{cases}$

12. **a** (iii)
   c (ii)
   b (i)
   d (iv)

Inequalities, Exercise 1. Page 46.

1. $(-4, 2) \cup (2, 5)$
2. $[-2, \infty)$
3. $(-5, -2) \cup [1, 4)$
4. $(-\infty, -6] \cup [-4, 3]$

Inequalities, Exercise 2. Page 49.

1. $(-1, \infty)$
2. $(-\infty, -2) \cup (-1, \infty)$
3. $[-2, -1]$
4. no solution
5. $x = 3$
6. $[2, 3]$
7. $(-\infty, -8.5) \cup (-4, 5) \cup (5, \infty)$
8. $(-\infty, -5] \cup [0, 4]$

Inequalities, Exercise 3. Page 50.

1. $(-\infty, -1) \cup (1, \infty)$
2. $(-1, \infty)$
3. $(-\infty, -4) \cup [-1, 1]$
4. $[-5, -\frac{3}{2})$
5. $(-\infty, -\frac{3}{2})$
6. $(-5, -3) \cup (-1, 1) \cup (3, 5)$

Solving Poly. & Rat.Functions, Exercise 1. Page 53.

1. $q(x) = x^3 + 3$
   $r(x) = x + 1$
2. $q(x) = 3x^2 - 5x$
   $r(x) = -6x^2 + 12x - 4$
3. $q(x) = x^2 - x + 1$
   $r(x) = 63$
4. $q(x) = x^3 + x^2 + x + 1$
   $r(x) = -x^2 + x - 4$
5. $q(x) = 4x^2 - 2x + 9$
   $r(x) = -4x + 17$
6. $q(x) = x^2 + 5$
   $r(x) = 0$
7. $q(x) = -x^2 + 1$
   $r(x) = 0$
8. $q(x) = x^2 - x + 1$
   $r(x) = 1$
9. $q(x) = 5x + 4$
   $r(x) = 0$
10. $q(x) = x^3 - 3x^2 + 9x - 27$
   $r(x) = 0$
11. $q(x) = x^3 + \frac{3}{4}x^2 + \frac{9}{16}x + \frac{107}{64}$
   $r(x) = -\frac{63}{64}$
12. $q(x) = \frac{5}{2}x^5 + \frac{5}{4}x^4 - \frac{5}{8}x^3 - \frac{39}{16}x^2 - \frac{29}{32}x + \frac{113}{64}$
   $r(x) = \frac{171}{64}x - \frac{305}{64}$
13. $q(x) = -2x^2 + 3x - 4$
   $r(x) = -7x + 7$
14. $q(x) = 0$
   $r(x) = 3x^2 - 2x - 1$
15. $q(x) = 5x^4 - 3x^2 + 7$
   $r(x) = 0$

Solving Poly. & Rat.Functions, Exercise 2. Page 56.

1. $q(x) = 4x^5 + 16x^4 + 28x^3 + 51x^2 + 105x + 207$
   $r(x) = 416$
2. $q(x) = 4x^5 - 4x^3 + 3x^2 - 3x + 3$
   $r = -4$
3. $q(x) = x^3 + 6x^2 + 9x + 31$
   $r(x) = 93$

4. $q(x) = 6x^2 - 7x + \frac{13}{2}$
   $r = -\frac{5}{4}$
5. $q(x) = 2x^4 - 6x^3 + 20x^2 - 64x + 192$
   $r = -569$
6. $q(x) = x^3 - 2x^2 + x$
   $r = 0$
7. $q(x) = 3x^3 - 5x^2 + 12x - 2$
   $r = 3$
8. $q(r) = 7x^3 + 4x^2 + x - 3$
   $r = -4$
9. $q(x) = x^3 - 2x^2 + 3x + 2$
   $r = 1$
10. 5856
11. -6144
12. 10
13. -3
14. -2
15. -13
16. 11
17. 0
18. 30

Solving Poly. & Rat.Functions, Exercise 3. Page 6

1. -1, 6
2. $-3, \sqrt{7}, -\sqrt{7}$
3. $\frac{1}{2}, -\frac{1}{2} - \frac{\sqrt{5}}{2}, -\frac{1}{2} + \frac{\sqrt{5}}{2}$
4. 3
5. -1, -2, -3
6. 5
7. $\frac{2}{3}$
8. 1, -2
9. 5, -5
10. No rational zeros. (At this stage, we have no method for determining whether there are any irrational real zeros, but the fact is that there aren't any.)
11. $1, -2, \frac{-5 + \sqrt{37}}{6}, \frac{-5 - \sqrt{37}}{6}$
12. -2, -5, 7

Solving Poly. & Rat.Functions, Exercise 4. Page 6

1. $1, -1, \sqrt{2}\,i, -\sqrt{2}\,i$
2. $-7, \frac{1}{5} + \frac{3}{5}i, \frac{1}{5} - \frac{3}{5}i$
3. $-1, 2 + 3i, 2 - 3i$
4. $2, 1 + 4i, 1 - 4i$
5. $-\frac{1}{2}, 3, 3i, -3i$
6. $\frac{4}{5}, -3, \frac{3}{2} - \frac{\sqrt{7}}{2}i, \frac{3}{2} + \frac{\sqrt{7}}{2}i$
7. $7, -7, 3 + \sqrt{19}, 3 - \sqrt{19}$
8. $-\frac{7}{5}, 2\sqrt{2}i, -2\sqrt{2}i$
9. 1, 2, -3, -4
10. $-\frac{1}{2}, \frac{1}{3}, -\frac{1}{2} + \frac{\sqrt{7}}{2}i, -\frac{1}{2} - \frac{\sqrt{7}}{2}i$

Solving Poly. & Rat.Functions, Exercise 5. Page 6

1. $(x-3)(x+13)$
2. $(x-3)^6(x+13)$
3. $-2(x-3)(x+13)$
4. $x(x+1)(x-2)$
5. $x^3(x+1)(x-2)$
6. $\frac{1}{2}x^3(x+1)(x-2)$
7. $(x-2)(x+3)(x-i)(x-(6-i))$ or
   $(x-2)(x+3)(x-i)(x-6+i)$

8. $(x-1)^2 (x-2)^3 (x+3) (x-6+i)$

9. x^2-x-2 **10.** x^3+2x^2-5x-6

11. $-\frac{1}{3}x^3 - \frac{2}{3}x^2 + \frac{5}{3}x + 2$

12. $x^3-8x^2+22x-20$ **13.** $x^4-10x^3+38x^2-64x+40$

14. $x^8-8x^7+41x^6$ **15.** $\frac{1}{2}x^8 - 4x^7 + \frac{25}{2}x^6$

16. $x^4-4x^3+41x^2-4x+40$ **17.** $(x-1)^2 (x-i) (x+i)$

18. $(x-3) (x+3) (x-(1+2i)) (x-(1-2i))$

19. $6(x-2) (x+1) (x-\frac{1}{2})$ **20.** $(x+2)^4$

21. $\frac{1}{3}(x-3)^3$

22. $3(x-1) (x-4) (x-(2+5i)) (x-(2-5i))$

Solving Poly. & Rat.Functions, Exercise 6. Page 68.

1. -1   **2.** none

3. 1   **4.** 3, $1+i$, $1-i$

5. 3   **6.** none

7. 0   **8.** -3

9. -1   **10.** $\frac{3}{2}$, -1

Solving Poly. & Rat.Functions, Exercise 7. Page 69.

1. 3, -4, 5; $(x-3) (x+4) (x-5)$

2. $-5+6i$, $-5-6i$; $(x-(-5+6i)) (x-(-5-6i))$ or
      $(x+5-6i) (x+5+6i)$

3. 2, 4, -1, -7; $(x-2) (x-4) (x+1) (x+7)$

4. -1, $\frac{4}{3}$, $-\frac{4}{3}$; $9(x+1)(x-\frac{4}{3})(x+\frac{4}{3})$

5. 2, $2i$, $-2i$; $(x-2)^3 (x-2i) (x+2i)$

6. $8, -4+\sqrt{27}, -4-\sqrt{27}, (x-8)(x+4-\sqrt{27})(x+4+\sqrt{27})$

7. 2, -5, $-\frac{1}{2}$, 0; $2x(x-2)(x+5)(x+\frac{1}{2})$

8. 5, $-\frac{1}{2}+\frac{3\sqrt{3}}{2}i$, $-\frac{1}{2}+\frac{3\sqrt{3}}{2}i$;

    $\frac{1}{2}(x-5)(x+\frac{1}{2}+\frac{3\sqrt{3}}{2}i)(x+\frac{1}{2}-\frac{3\sqrt{3}}{2}i)$

9. 2; $\dfrac{(x-2)^3(x-2i)(x+2i)}{(x-2i)(x+2i)}$

10. 1, $-\frac{1}{2}+\frac{\sqrt{3}}{2}i$, $-\frac{1}{2}-\frac{\sqrt{3}}{2}i$;

    $\dfrac{(x-1)(x+\frac{1}{2}+\frac{\sqrt{3}}{2}i)(x+\frac{1}{2}-\frac{\sqrt{3}}{2}i)}{(x-2)(x+1-\sqrt{3}i)(x+1+\sqrt{3}i)}$

11. $-5+6i$, $-5-6i$

12. -1, $\frac{4}{3}$, $-\frac{4}{3}$

13. 8, $-4+3\sqrt{3}$, $-4-3\sqrt{3}$

14. 5, $-\frac{1}{2}+\frac{3\sqrt{3}}{2}i$, $-\frac{1}{2}-\frac{3\sqrt{3}}{2}i$

15. $1, -\frac{1}{2}+\frac{\sqrt{3}}{2}i, -\frac{1}{2}-\frac{\sqrt{3}}{2}i$

Graphing Poly. & Rat.Functs., Exercise 1. Page 76.

1.

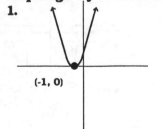

(-1, 0)

2.

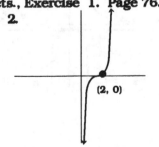

(2, 0)

3.

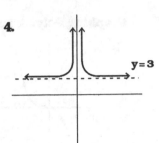

4.

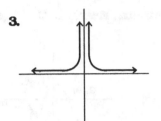

y=3

5.

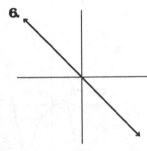

$(0,\frac{1}{2})$

6.

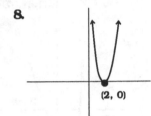

7.

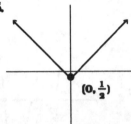

(0, 2)

8.

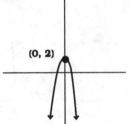

(2, 0)

9.

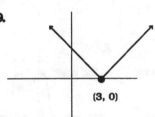

(3, 0)

10.

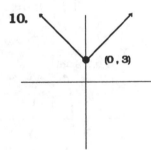

(0 , 3)

11a.

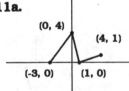

(0, 4)   (4, 1)

(-3, 0)   (1, 0)

11b.

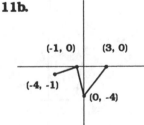

(-1, 0)   (3, 0)

(-4, -1)   (0, -4)

11c.

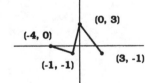

(0, 3)

(-4, 0)

(-1, -1)   (3, -1)

11d.

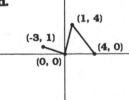

(1, 4)

(-3, 1)   (4, 0)

(0, 0)

147

1.

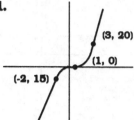

(3, 20)

(1, 0)

(-2, 15)

2.

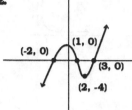

(-2, 0)   (1, 0)

(3, 0)

(2, -4)

3.

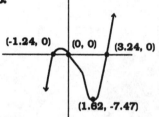

(-1.24, 0)   (0, 0)   (3.24, 0)

(1.62, -7.47)

4.

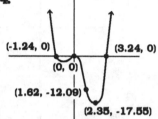

(-1.24, 0)   (3.24, 0)

(0, 0)

(1.62, -12.09)

(2.35, -17.55)

5.

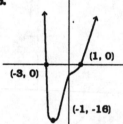

(1, 0)

(-3, 0)

(-1, -16)

6.

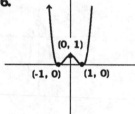

(0, 1)

(-1, 0)   (1, 0)

7.

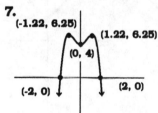

(-1.22, 6.25)   (1.22, 6.25)

(0, 4)

(-2, 0)   (2, 0)

8.

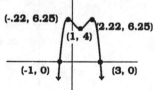

(-.22, 6.25)   (2.22, 6.25)

(1, 4)

(-1, 0)   (3, 0)

9.

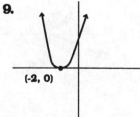

(-2, 0)

10.

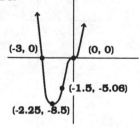

(-3, 0)   (0, 0)

(-1.5, -5.06)

(-2.25, -8.5)

1.

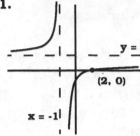

y = 1

(2, 0)

x = -1

2.

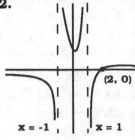

(2, 0)

x = -1   x = 1

3.

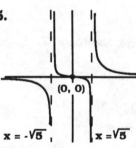

(-√2, 0)   (√2, 0)

x = -1   x = 1

4.

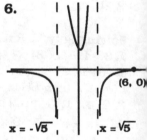

y = x +

x = 2

5.

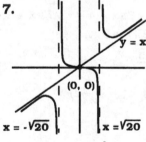

(0, 0)

x = -√5   x = √5

6.

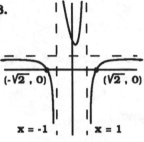

(6, 0)

x = -√5   x = √5

7.

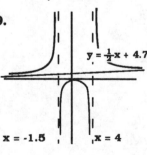

y = x

(0, 0)

x = -√20   x = √20

8.

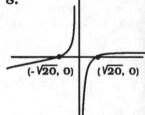

(-√20, 0)   (√20, 0)

9.

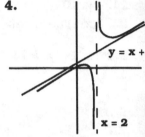

$y = \frac{1}{2}x + 4.75$

x = -1.5   x = 4

10.

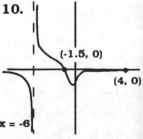

(-1.5, 0)

(4, 0)

x = -6

11.

y = 2.5

(-2, 0)   (0.4, 0)

x = -4   x = 3.5

12.

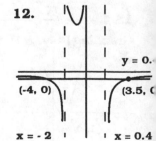

y = 0.

(-4, 0)   (3.5, 0

x = -2   x = 0.4

148

Trigonometric Functions, Exercise 1, Page 97.

1. sin = -0.6, cos = 0.8, tan = -0.75, sec = 1.25,
csc = -1.67, tan = -1.33.

2. sin = -0.814, cos = -0.581, tan = 1.400, sec = -1.720,
csc = -1.229, cot = 0.714.

3. sin = 0.809, cos = 0.588, tan = 1.375, sec = 1.700,
csc = 1.236, cot = 0.727.

4. sin = 0, cos = -1, tan = 0, sec = -1, csc = undefined,
cot = undefined.

5. QIII   **6.** QIV

7. 60°   **8.** 25°

9. 10°

10. sin = -0.966, cos = -0.259, tan = 3.732, sec = -3.861,
csc = -1.035, cot = 0.268.

11. sin = -0.555, cos = 0.832, tan = -0.667, sec = 1.202,
csc = -1.803, cot = -1.500.

12. sin = 1, cos = 0, tan = undefined, sec = undefined,
csc = 1, cot = 0.

Trigonometric Functions, Exercise 2, Page 100.

1. $\frac{2\pi}{9}$ **2.** $-\frac{11\pi}{4}$

3. 135°   **4.** $-\frac{108}{\pi}$

5. $\frac{\sqrt{3}}{2}$ **6.** $-\frac{1}{\sqrt{2}}$

7. $\frac{1}{\sqrt{3}}$ **8.** undefined

9. $\frac{2}{\sqrt{3}}$ **10.** undefined

Trigonometric Functions, Exercise 3, Page 105.

1. 3   **2.** undefined

3. $\frac{\pi}{4}$ **4.** $\frac{3\pi}{4}$

5. $-\frac{\pi}{4}$ **6.** $\frac{4}{5}$

7. $\frac{3}{5}$ **8.** 0

9. 0   **10.** $\frac{\sqrt{41}}{5}$

Trigonometric Functions, Exercise 4, Page 111.

1.

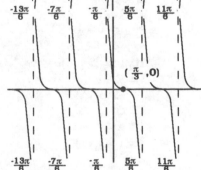

2.

3.

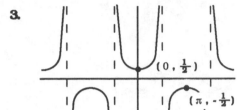

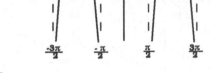

4.

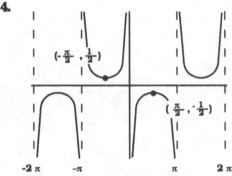

5.

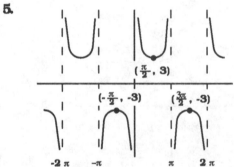

6.

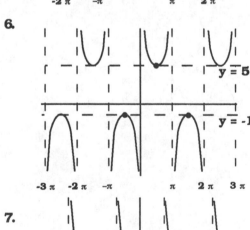

7.

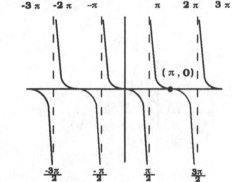

8.

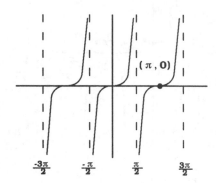

9.

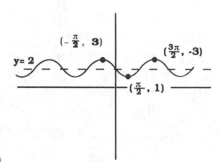

10.

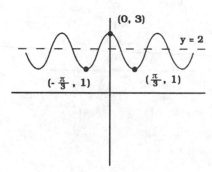

11.

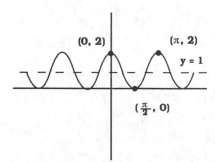

12.

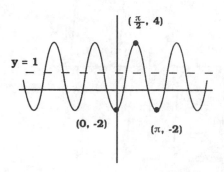

Trigonometric Functions, Exercise 5, Page 114.

1. $\sin x$	**2.** $\cos x$
3. 0	**4.** $\tan^2 y$
5. 1	**6.** $\sec x$
7. 1	**8.** $2\sec^2 A$
9. $-\cos x$	**10.** $\sec y$

Trigonometric Functions, Exercise 6, Page 120.

1. $2 - \sqrt{3}$ **2.** $\frac{\sqrt{3}+1}{2\sqrt{2}}$ or $\frac{\sqrt{6}+\sqrt{2}}{4}$

3. $\frac{-1-\sqrt{3}}{2\sqrt{2}}$ or $\frac{-\sqrt{2}-\sqrt{6}}{4}$ **4.** $\frac{3\sqrt{7}-12}{20}$

5. $-\frac{1}{\sqrt{5}}$ **6.** $\frac{-12-3\sqrt{7}}{9-4\sqrt{7}}$ or $\frac{192+75\sqrt{7}}{31}$

7. $-\frac{25}{7}$ **8.** $-\sin x$

9. $\sin x$ **10.** $\tan x$

11. $\cos 2A$ **12.** $2\cot^2 y$

Trigonometric Functions, Exercise 7, Page 123.

1. $-\frac{\pi}{3}, \frac{\pi}{3}$ **2.** $-\frac{2\pi}{3}, -\frac{\pi}{3}, \frac{\pi}{3}, \frac{2\pi}{3}$

3. $240°, 360°$ **4.** $\frac{\pi}{6}, \frac{2\pi}{3}, \frac{7\pi}{6}, \frac{5\pi}{3}$

5. $-135°, 0°, 45°$ **6.** no solution

7. π **8.** no solution

9. $-\pi, 0, \pi$ **10.** $161.565°, 341.565°, 45°, 225$

11. $\frac{\pi}{2} + 2n\pi, \frac{3\pi}{2} + 2n\pi$ **12.** $40.893 + 180°n$

$139.107 + 180°n$

(or $-40.893 + 180°n$)

Expon. & Logar. Functions., Exercise 1, Page 126.

1. a. >	**2. a.** 0
b. <	**b.** 5
c. >	**c.** no solution
d. <	**d.** no solution
e. >	

Expon. & Logar. Functions., Exercise 2, Page 128.

1. 4	**2.** 5
3. two solutions: $0, \frac{1}{2}$	**4.** no solution
5. 0	**6.** 0
7. -3	**8.** no solution
9. $\frac{10}{3}$	**10.** 5

Expon. & Logar. Functions., Exercise 3, Page 131.

1. $3^y = x$	**2.** $x^3 = y$
3. $y^3 = x - 2$	**4.** $5^{x-2} = y$
5. $(x-1)^6 = y + 4$	**6.** $\log_4 y = x$
7. $\log_y x = 4$	**8.** $\log_{(y-1)} x = 4$
9. $\log_x 7 = y + 2$	**10.** $\log_6(2y-4) = x - 3$
11. 1.1761	**12.** 0.9176
13. -12.489	**14.** -2.5702
15. 1.6131	**16.** 0
17. no solution	**18.** $x = 7$
19. $\log_6 8$	**20.** $\log_{0.8}(7)$

Expon. & Logar. Functions., Exercise 4, Page 133 .

1.
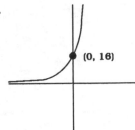
(0, 16)

2.
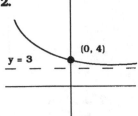
y = 3   (0, 4)

3.
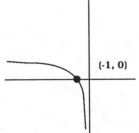
(-1, 0)

4.
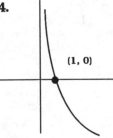
(1, 0)

5.
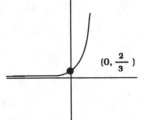
$(0, \frac{2}{3})$

6.
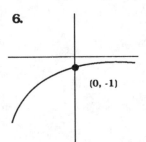
(0, -1)

7.
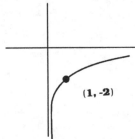
(1, -2)

8.
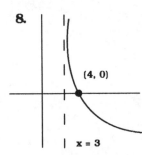
(4, 0)

x = 3

9.
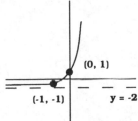
(0, 1)

(-1, -1)   y = -2

10.
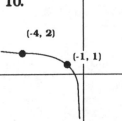
(-4, 2)

(-1, 1)

11.
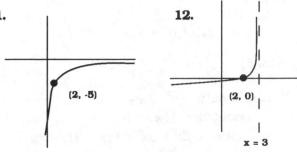
(2, -5)

12.

(2, 0)

x = 3

Expon. & Logar. Functions., Exercise 5, Page 135 .

1. $2\log_b x - \frac{1}{2}\log_b y$ **2.** $\log_b x + 2\log_b y + 3\log_b z$

3. no simplification possible **4.** $b\log_b x$

5. $\log_b \frac{x^3\sqrt{z}}{y^2}$ **6.** $\log_b y^x$

7. $\log_b \frac{y}{x^3}$ **8.** $\log_b x^5$

9. 0.3211 **10.** 0.7704

11. 2.95975 **12.** 0.74805

Expon. & Logar. Functions., Exercise 6, Page 138.

1. $x = \frac{3}{2}$ **2.** x=0.8702

3. x=0.8580 **4.** x=1.7449

5. x=-0.7449 **6.** x=1.0296

7. x=81 **8.** x=3

9. x=24 **10.** $x = \frac{3\pm\sqrt{5}}{2}$, 2.618 or 0.382

11. x=5 **12.** x=48

Expon. & Logar. Functions., Exercise 7, Page 141 .

1. 16,900 **2.** 36.45 years

3. 25,044,246 **4.** 1926 or 1927 (26.8 yrs)

5. 7.72 grams **6.** 78.87 days

7. 16.2 days ago **8.** 93

Final Assessment Test, Page 142.

1. -2   1.654321   -999.3   0   2.99999

2. $\frac{20}{3}$, -8

3. $x^{-\frac{8}{5}}$

4. $f(x) = \sqrt{x + 4}$

5. a. $x^2 + x - 2$ **b.** $x^2 - x - 4$

  c. $x^3 + x^2 - 3x - 3$ **d.** $\frac{x^2 - 3}{x+1}$

  e. $x^2 + 2x - 2$ **f.** $x^2 - 2$

  g. $x^2 - 4x + 1$ **h.** 14

6. $(-3, 0) \cup (0, \infty)$

7. a. 1
  b. -1
  c. $(-\infty, \ -1] \cup (0, \ \infty)$

8. $(3, 8]$

9. a. quotient: $3x^3 + 5x + 1$
    remainder: $11x - 7$
  b. quotient: $3x^4 - 6x^3 + 11x^2 - 21x + 43$
    remainder: -95

10. a. $(x - 3)(x + 3)(x - (2 + 3i))(x - (2 - 3i))$

  b.

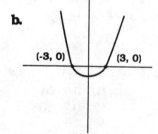

11.

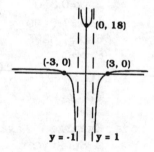

12. $\sin = \dfrac{-7}{\sqrt{65}}$ $\cos = \dfrac{4}{\sqrt{65}}$

   $\tan = \dfrac{-7}{4}$ $\sec = \dfrac{\sqrt{65}}{4}$

   $\csc = \dfrac{-\sqrt{65}}{7}$ $\cot = \dfrac{-4}{7}$

13.

14. $\sec^4 y$

15. $\dfrac{2 - \frac{2}{\sqrt{21}}}{1 + \frac{4}{\sqrt{21}}}$, or $10 - 2\sqrt{21}$

16.

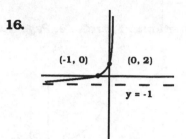

17. a. $x^y = 4$
  b. $\log_{13} k = x - 1$

18. a. 3
  b. -0.2

Math Series

The Straight Forward Math Series

is systematic, first diagnosing skill levels, then *practice*, periodic *review*, and *testing*.

Blackline

GP-006 Addition
GP-012 Subtraction
GP-007 Multiplication
GP-013 Division
GP-039 Fractions
GP-083 Word Problems, Book 1

The Advanced Straight Forward Math Series

is a higher level system to diagnose, practice, review, and test skills.

Blackline

GP-015 Advanced Addition
GP-016 Advanced Subtraction
GP-017 Advanced Multiplication
GP-018 Advanced Division
GP-020 Advanced Decimals
GP-021 Advanced Fractions
GP-044 Mastery Tests
GP-028 Pre-Algebra, Book 1
GP-029 Pre-Algebra, Book 2
GP-030 Pre-Geometry, Book 1
GP-031 Pre-Geometry, Book 2

Large Editions

Blackline

GP-037 Algebra, Book 1
GP-038 Algebra, Book 2
GP-045 Trigonometry
GP-054 Geometry
GP-053 Pre-Calculus
GP-064 Calculus AB, Vol. 1
GP-067 Calculus AB, Vol. 2

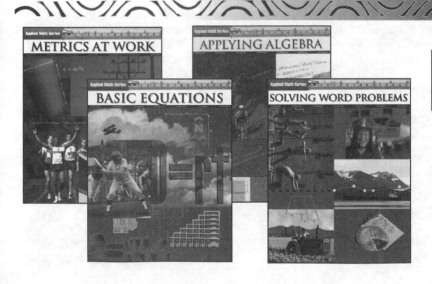

Applied Math Series

The Applied Math Series

is designed for those who wonder how various mathematic disciplines can be used to solve everyday problems.

GP-063 Applying Algebra
GP-070 Metrics at Work
GP-080 Solving Word Problems
GP-084 Basic Equations

English Series

The Straight Forward English Series

is designed to measure, teach, review, and master specified English skills: capitalization and punctuation; nouns and pronouns; verbs; adjectives and adverbs; prepositions, conjunctions and interjections; sentences; clauses and phrases, and mechanics.

Each workbook is a simple, straightforward approach to learning English skills. Skills are keyed to major school textbook adoptions.

Pages are reproducible.

GP-032   Capitalization and Punctuation
GP-033   Nouns and Pronouns
GP-034   Verbs
GP-035   Adjectives and Adverbs
GP-041   Sentences
GP-043   Prepositions, conjunctions,
          & Interjections

Advanced Series

Large editions

GP-055   Clauses & Phrases
GP-056   Mechanics
GP-075   Grammar & Diagramming
          Sentences

Discovering Literature Series

The Discovering Literature Series

is designed to develop an appreciation for literature and to improve reading skills. Each guide in the series features an award winning novel and explores a wide range of critical reading skills and literature elements.

GP-076   A Teaching Guide to My Side of the Mountain
GP-077   A Teaching Guide to Where the Red Fern Grows
GP-078   A Teaching Guide to Mrs. Frisby & the Rats of NIMH
GP-079   A Teaching Guide to Island of the Blue Dolphins
GP-093   A Teaching Guide to the Outsiders
GP-094   A Teaching Guide to Roll of Thunder

Challenging Level

GP-090   The Hobbit: A Teaching Guide
GP-091   Redwall: A Teaching Guide
GP-092   The Odyssey: A Teaching Guide
GP-097   The Giver: A Teaching Guide
GP-096   Lord of the Flies: A Teaching Guide
GP-074   To Kill A Mockingbird: A Teaching Guide